THE
COOKBOOK NOTEBOOK

THE
COOKBOOK NOTEBOOK

WITH ILLUSTRATIONS BY
EDWARD BAWDEN

WRITTEN BY MAGDA JOICEY
WITH NOTES BY ANGELA CARTER

UNICORN

CONTENTS

A FEW
GENERAL HINTS

A Few General Hints

❖ Many soups and stews are improved by the addition of herbs. If you can easily get fresh ones, tie a sprig of thyme, parsley, marjoram and bay leaf into a 'bouquet' and remove before serving. However, mixed dried herbs, which you can easily get in a packet do very well instead of the fresh ones. You can leave marjoram out of the 'bouquet' if it is unprocurable. The addition of a little grated nutmeg is a great improvement to most minced chicken, ham or rabbit dishes.

❖ A little sugar should be added to both tomato salads and cooked tomatoes, unless you are using the very best ones.

❖ Lemon and cooking sherry can usually be substituted for white wine.

❖ Always boil fish in water to which a little vinegar and some herbs have been added.

❖ Do not let egg sauces boil or they will curdle. Always use peppercorns and a pepper mill. I use black pepper myself, but that is a question of taste. Never add pepper to soups, stews, etc., until a short time before serving.

❖ Some of the best suet is from around a sheep's kidney. The suet from one kidney is usually enough to make a pudding for four people.

❖ Instead of tying up steamed puddings with a cloth and greased paper, you can use a small plate with a weight on the top.

❖ While butter is short you can use a mixture of margarine and lard in all cakes and pastry. Margarine alone can be used in cakes, but it makes them a little dry; on the other hand, lard alone makes delicious pastry. Do not try to fry in margarine, or to grease cake tins or pudding basins with it, as the ingredients will stick.

❖ When you use dried eggs in cakes or puddings reconstitute them first, then, in most cases, they are just as good as fresh ones.

❖ Rabbit can be used instead of chicken in most made-up dishes.

❖ When making an open tart or flan which is to be baked without a filling always prick the bottom to prevent it rising. A few dried peas or lentils can be put in the bottom to answer the same purpose. They can be used over and over again.

❖ Except where specifically stated to the contrary these recipes are for three or four people.

A FEW BASIC
RECIPES

Boiled Rice

Put a handful of rice per head in a large saucepan full of fast-boiling salted water. Boil until the rice is cooked, 10 -15 minutes. Be careful not to overcook; try a few grains from time to time to make sure. Pour into a colander and strain. Now hold the colander under the cold tap and wash well until every grain is separate. Put the saucepan lid over the rice and steam over a saucepan of fast-boiling water to reheat.

◆ ❖ ◆

Rice is a carbohydrate, or energy food. In its natural state it contains Vitamin B, the vitamin that protects us from nervous disorders. Unfortunately, the modern preference for a highly polished grain means that this vitamin is lost because it is the husk of the rice grain that contains it, and this is removed in the polishing process.

While we are on the subject of rice, I must mention that the secret of a really creamy rice pudding is to blanche the rice (1½ ozs. to 1 pint of milk) with boiling water before adding the milk, and then to stir the pudding three times during the first half-hour of baking – in other words, stir off three skins – try a bay leaf as flavouring for a change. Plain boiled rice makes a good and simple sweet served with boiled raisins and black treacle.

Short Pastry

8 ozs. self-raising flour
4 ozs. butter or 2 ozs. margarine/butter and 2 ozs. lard

Sieve the flour into a bowl. Mix in the fat with your fingers until the whole is like fine breadcrumbs. Add sufficient cold water to make into a stiff paste, mixing with a knife. Roll out very thin on a floured board. Bake in a hot oven.

For a super-rich crust use a yolk of egg for mixing, and add a dessertspoon of caster sugar. Don't have your paste too stiff or it will be tough. Knead lightly until free from cracks for a smooth surface. Short crust should only be rolled once with sharp light strokes in one direction. To give a smart appearance, glaze savoury dishes with beaten egg and sweet dishes with cold water or milk, and dredge with caster sugar. For richer sweets, remove when nearly baked and brush over with lightly beaten white of egg and dredge with caster sugar, return to oven for a few minutes, this gives a 'meringue' glaze.

Suet Crust

8 ozs. self-raising flour
4 ozs. chopped suet

Mix the sieved flour and the suet in a bowl. Add sufficient cold water to make a very soft dough. Suet crust can be made one day and boiled the next. It does not hurt by keeping.

Shredded suet is the most convenient to use, but it is more economical to buy fresh suet from the butcher. Suet is the inside fat of the ox and sheep, it acts as a cushion for the delicate organs of the stomach, and is easily recognisable from other fat because it is not joined to the flesh. Beef suet is softer and more digestible than mutton suet, which is more suitable for frying than for puddings and suet crust. A piece of suet can be kept indefinitely in the flour bin if it is quite dry and clean. Fresh suet should be sweet and firm, free from kernels or any discolouration or blood streaks. This suet crust recipe can be made into a delicious pudding by substituting 2 ozs. (½ breakfast cup) of fresh breadcrumbs for 2 ozs. of the flour, mixing to a fairly stiff dough with cold water (⅓ pint) and steaming in a greased basin for 1½-2 hours. Serve with jam or syrup.

Rough Puff Pastry

8 ozs. self-raising flour
½ teaspoon salt
6 ozs. butter or 2 ozs. margarine/butter and 4 ozs. lard

Sieve the flour into a bowl, add the salt and mix well. Cut the fat into small pieces and mix into the flour. Now add sufficient cold water to make a fairly soft dough. Roll into an oblong shape on a floured board. Fold in three. Turn the other way and roll into the same shape again. Repeat until all the fat is absorbed. Be careful to keep the corners square at each rolling. Bake in a hot oven.

◆ ❖ ◆

I always use plain flour for flaky pastries because self-raising flour contains a raising agent which causes the dough to expand rather like a sponge. With flaky pastry, the expansion should be between the thin layers of paste, and this results from the numerous rolling and folding of the dough. A teaspoon of lemon juice added to the water for mixing tends to counteract the richness, and make the pastry light. Don't have your lumps of fat smaller than a walnut or you'll probably find you have a short crust instead of a flaky one. Another tip is to reserve a little of the flour from the 8 ozs. for dredging; if you use additional flour you'll put your proportions out.

Always keep everything as cold as possible in pastry making, because the cooler the air entrapped in the dough the greater will be the expansion in the oven, and the lighter the pastry. If possible, let your pastry stand in a cold place (a refrigerator is best) for at least 10 minutes before cutting out; this allows for shrinkage and firms up the fat. Rough Puff paste should be rolled and folded four times.

Brown Breadcrumbs

For any recipe that does not require fresh breadcrumbs. Cut stale bread into slices or break into small pieces. Bake slowly in the oven until dry right through. Put on a pastry board and roll with a rolling pin until the crumbs are of the required fineness.

Here's a nice job for a little daughter – rolling the dry bread into crumbs makes the sort of noise children delight in, and it keeps them out of mischief. For a professional finish to an egg-and-crumb coating, sieve the crumbs for evenness. They will keep indefinitely if stored in a covered jar.

Stock

Onions
Carrots
Beef and/or veal bones and trimmings
Mixed herbs
Salt, pepper
Vegetable water

Slice the vegetables. Put all the ingredients in a large pan. Cover with vegetable water (if you have no vegetable water use plain cold water). Boil rapidly and skim until no more scum rises. Simmer for 2 or 3 hours. Unless you have an Aga or Esse you can just simmer when convenient and take off the heat in between times. Strain off the liquid. When cold, skim the fat off the top. Always take the lid off the pan when the stock is cooked or it will go sour.

◆ ❖ ◆

For good stock, absolute cleanliness of utensils is essential. Each ingredient must be perfectly fresh and free from taint. Never put fat, cabbage, cooked vegetables, or anything starchy like bread and thickened sauces into the stock-pot or the stock will be cloudy. An earthenware casserole or marmite is best for a small family, the inside glaze renders it non-absorbent, and the lid prevents evaporation. To every 1 lb. of bones add 2 qts. of water. Boil until the bones are dry and pitted with holes. Don't skim off the brown scum as this is coagulated protein, white scum consists of impurities. Boil up stock every day in hot weather and every second day in winter to prevent souring.

Pot Roast

If you are only two and want a very small joint (e.g., a small piece of best end of lamb, or a fillet of beef) you can roast it in a pot. Take just a little longer than the 20 minutes per pound plus twenty minutes over for lamb, and 15 minutes per pound plus 15 minutes over for beef. You should melt a little fat in an iron saucepan before putting in the joint and cook over medium heat. Joints cooked in this way are not as good as those roasted in the oven, as the steam makes them taste rather like a stew, but they are, of course, economical if you do not want to use the oven.

◆ ❖ ◆

Apart from economy in fuel, pot roasting is economical in money too, for a cheaper cut of meat such as topside or chuck rib of beef, or middle or scrag end of mutton, can be made tender and succulent by this method of cooking. It is a good idea to bone the joint. Get the butcher to do it for you or you can do it yourself with a little practice and a sharp pointed knife. A savoury stuffing will give more flavour to the joint and make it go further. Remember the nutritional value of meat is the same whether it is sirloin or oxtail. See that all sides of the meat are browned in the fat before leaving your pot roast to cook. This seals in the juices and improves the flavour. A really well-fitting lid is a necessity, and you should baste occasionally, turning the joint to ensure even cooking.

Hard-Boiled Eggs

Put the eggs in a covered saucepan of cold water, bring to the boil and simmer for 10 minutes. Take out and plunge into cold water; stand for a few minutes. They will now peel quite easily.

If you peel the eggs under water the unpleasant sulphur smell will be avoided. Reconstituted dried egg steamed until firm can be cut into fancy shapes when cold and used as a garnish for a clear soup. A hard-boiled egg is the base of innumerable savouries. Cut in half, remove yolk and pound it up with any flavouring you fancy – anchovy essence is a classic, or use grated cheese, chopped cooked mushrooms, tomato purée, a little cooked fish, moistened with cream and well seasoned – the possibilities are endless. Return the mixture to the whites and serve on rounds of fried bread or toast.

Tomatoes to Peel

Put in a basin, cover with boiling water, stand for a minute. They will now peel quite easily.

Tomatoes are rich in Vitamins C (the anti-scorbutic vitamin) and A, which is essential to maintain the body in a healthy state. These vitamins escape into the air when the skin is broken, so don't slice the tomatoes until the last moment. It is often difficult to dish up cooked tomatoes looking tidy, however the following method is fairly foolproof. Cut in half, place in a greased tin, dredge with pepper and salt, put a small piece of fat on each half, cover with greased paper and bake in a moderate oven for 5-10 minutes.

SOUPS

Cauliflower Soup

1 small cauliflower
1½ pints milk
2 tablespoons flour
Salt, pepper
A small piece of butter

Boil the cauliflower until rather overcooked in about two inches of water. Keep the water, remove the leaves and mash up the rest of the cauliflower with a fork. Mix the flour carefully with a little milk so that there are no lumps. Now put the cauliflower and the water it has been cooked in back into the saucepan with the milk and flour mixture strained into it and the rest of the milk. Season well and cook until it is thick, stirring frequently. Add a knob or two of butter just before serving.

◆ ❖ ◆

Dietetically, the use of milk in this soup makes it a nourishing addition to a meal that need only contain a light second course. The fact that the cauliflower has to be fairly soft – i.e. 'rather overcooked' would destroy the Vitamin C content, as this element is soluble in boiling water and escapes in steam. I would therefore suggest a garnish of freshly chopped parsley added at the last moment to make up the loss. Alternately, remove the green leaves before cooking, chop them, and add to the briskly boiling water for the last 5 minutes of cooking, drain and use as a garnish. This soup would be good with sandwiches for a light supper.

Leek and Potato Soup

4 leeks
6 medium size potatoes
2 pints chicken stock
2 tablespoons butter
2 tablespoons flour
1 teaspoon chopped chives
2 or 3 tablespoons of cream (optional)

Cut the white part of the leeks into fairly small pieces and fry in butter until golden brown. Add flour and blend well, then add the stock. Add the potatoes sliced rather thin and some salt to taste. Cook for three-quarters of an hour, then strain. Add cream just before serving and sprinkle with finely cut chives. Less extravagant and almost as good – use two Oxo cubes and water instead of chicken stock.

Leeks are tricky things to wash – the best way is to cut them in half longwise, and wash under a running tap or leave for a few minutes in salted water. Margarine or dripping can be used for sautéing the leeks if butter is short. Remember to dry them well before adding to the hot fat, or they will spit like fury while they are frying. When you want to leave a pan on the stove for long slow-cooking without mishap, use an asbestos mat, or if you are using an electric stove, stand the pan half off the hot plate at its lowest switch, but remember occasionally to turn the pan so that each side has its share of the heat.

Marrow Soup

1 medium size marrow
2 onions
A piece of butter the size of an egg
4 or 5 tomatoes
A few pieces of bacon or bacon rind
Celery salt, pepper
1 pint milk and if possible a little cream

Peel the marrow, remove the seeds and chop coarsely; chop the onions and peel the tomatoes. Put them all together in a saucepan. Fill about half-way up the vegetables with water, and simmer for about 2 hours. Add the bacon or rind and the seasoning, and cook a further half hour. Remove bacon or rind and add the milk. Heat again, add a little cream if you can spare it, and serve. This soup can easily be made beforehand and reheated.

This is a delicious soup, and is an excellent medium for using up those marrows that have passed their prime. The tomatoes can be on the ripe side too. If butter isn't forthcoming use margarine or, preferably, pork dripping, though this may make the soup a little on the rich side for some people. Dietetically, its use is more of a stimulant than a food, but the addition of a parsley or watercress garnish would give it Vitamin C, and I suggest small squares of toast as an accompaniment.

Minestrone

Take 2 pints of vegetable stock or a pint of vegetable stock and a pint of water; add 2 or 3 beef or veal bones, boil fast and skim. Now add 2 or 3 sliced carrots, a chopped onion, a few chopped cabbage leaves, a dessertspoon of mixed herbs, salt, celery salt and pepper to taste. Simmer for half an hour, add a handful of chopped macaroni and simmer for another half-hour or so. Remove the bones and served.

Contrary to popular belief, there is not much nutritional value in bone stock. The fact that liquid sets into a firm jelly after long boiling of bones proves very little, as only a minute quantity of gelatine (1%) is necessary to set a liquid, and it is the gelatine content of connective tissue of meat that, with the myosin (the protein content of the muscle of the animal), provides body building material. But I am straying from Minestrone. What I meant to say was that a clear soup has little food value, it is the additions – in this case, the macaroni and vegetables – that make it body fuel. Grated cheese, which is concentrated protein, can be served with Minestrone, and this makes it one of the most nourishing soups there are.

Mushroom Soup

½ lb. mushrooms
1 pint milk
1 tablespoon oatmeal
Salt, pepper
A small piece of butter or a few tablespoons of cream

Peel and chop the mushrooms (stalks will do very well for soup). Simmer them for half an hour in a pint of water, add the milk and bring to the boil. Sprinkle in the oatmeal carefully so that it does not go lumpy, and cook for a further quarter of an hour, stirring from time to time. Just before serving add a small lump of butter or, preferably, a few tablespoons of cream.

◆ ❖ ◆

The use of oatmeal as a thickener adds nutritional value to the soup because it contains a very high percentage of protein – actually 12%. A mushroom soup is essentially a 'de luxe' affair so use fine oatmeal instead of the more common medium ground, or you will not have that smooth creaminess that is called for. As a 'play safe' for the inexperienced, I suggest creaming the oatmeal with a little of the milk, and then blending with the rest of the liquid, carefully, using a wooden spoon. If, instead of fresh milk you use a tin of evaporated and half a pint of water, your soup will have a deliciously rich flavour without butter or cream.

Spinach Soup

1½ pints spinach water
1 pint milk
2 tablespoons oatmeal
A little fresh spinach
Salt, pepper
A small piece of butter

Boil the spinach water until it is reduced to 1 pint. Add the milk and boil up together. Mix the oatmeal to a paste with a little cold water, pour on the boiling liquid. Return to the heat and simmer for 6 minutes, stirring all the time (or you can use a double saucepan). Season and add a few finely chopped spinach leaves and a small piece of butter. Boil another 2 minutes and serve.

Here is another soup for the gourmet. If you find 1½ pints of spinach water difficult to come by, cook 2 lbs. of spinach until tender, with no water other than that remaining on the leaves after washing in five waters, press through a fine sieve and make up the resulting liquid to 1½ pints with water or white stock. I always add a few stalks of celery while cooking this soup, removing them before serving, as I find this enriches the flavour. Spinach soup supplies Vitamin C. Remember the darker the green, the richer the Vitamin C content of vegetables. Serve croûtes of fried bread with this soup.

Sorrel Soup

2 pints milk
6 ozs. sago (or semolina)
2 handsful sorrel leaves
A lump of butter the size of an egg
Salt, pepper

Boil the milk, add the sago or semolina and seasoning, and simmer until cooked. Meanwhile fold over the sorrel leaves and remove the central stalk, chop and cook gently in the butter. Add to the milk etc. and simmer for a few minutes. Sorrel can be bought in one or two French shops in Soho or if you have a garden you can grow it yourself, it is quite easy to grow. The slightly acidic flavour makes a great change from other green vegetables.

Here is something really unusual. Sorrel was in common use until the beginning of this century, and only faded out of favour with the growing dependence on the greengrocer's shop and the gradual decline of the kitchen garden. Sorrel is a weed, and the vegetable grower didn't bother to cultivate it and hadn't the labour to collect it from the fields. As a child I loved the sharp flavour but found it had dire results on one occasion when, after gorging myself on a particularly abundant plant, I was tied up with colic for several days afterwards! However, don't let that alarm you, the quantity given in this recipe could be nothing but beneficial.

Tomato and Onion Soup

2 lbs. tomatoes
2 small or 1 large onion
A knob of butter
Salt, pepper
1 pint creamy milk
1 or 2 spoonful cream (optional)

Not a very elegant-looking, but a very delicious soup, and much less trouble to make than the usual kind! Skin the tomatoes, chop the onions. Melt the butter in a saucepan, add the onions, and cook until a golden brown; now add the tomatoes cut in half and cook with the lid on until the mixture is quite soft. Season and add a touch of sugar if required (it depends on the flavour of the tomatoes). Pour in the milk and cream and heat up, but do not boil again as the tomato is apt to curdle the milk. You need not use the best tomatoes for this soup, so although it takes rather a lot of them they can be the cheapest ones!

◆ ❖ ◆

I adapt this recipe in this way for a change: blend two level tablespoons of flour with the milk, boil for 3 minutes, cool a little, and add the tomato mixture sieved when quite soft; season just before serving, and add a good pinch of celery salt, a dessertspoon of sugar and a dash of vinegar. If you can spare cream or top of milk, add a little to the plates after pouring out the soup and serve with fried croûtes. This is a good mid-morning drink instead of coffee, and we often have it on Sunday evenings, followed by celery and cheese and biscuits. While on the subject of tomatoes, for hot weather, dilute bottled tomato juice with top of milk or thin cream, add a dash of Worcester sauce, chill and serve in cocktail glasses, with hand-made cheese straws (see page 32).

Vegetable Soup

1 onion
½ medium-size cabbage
1 stick celery
3 potatoes
3 carrots
1 dessertspoon mixed herbs
1 bay leaf
Salt, pepper and celery salt to taste
2 pints water

Chop all the vegetables coarsely; put all the ingredients into a large saucepan with the water and bring to the boil. Simmer for 1½ to 2 hours. Remove the bay leaf and serve. It is best to grind the pepper in only about half an hour before serving.

This recipe might be called 'Cook's standby' – it is excellent made with the ingredients in the recipe, but any root vegetables can be used, with the exception of beetroot, bearing in mind that no one flavour should predominate. Dietetically, this provides bulk to the menu and will satisfy, though the food value is low. It could be enriched with cheese and oatmeal dumplings, and a sprinkling of freshly chopped parsley.

ENTRÉES AND SAVOURIES

Cheese Straws

4 ozs. self-raising flour
2 ozs. cheese (mixed Parmesan and Gruyere is best)
2 ozs. fat
Salt, pepper, a touch of cayenne

Mix as for short pastry (see page 13), then add the cheese (grated) and seasoning. Roll out and cut into straws. Bake until golden brown in a hottish oven and serve hot. Cheese straws can be reheated but they are not quite so nice. You can make a little ring for each person and put the straws through it. You can also make with rough puff pastry (see page 15) if preferred.

I would suggest mixing the cheese into the fat and flour before adding the cold water drop by drop – very little should be necessary. Beware of overcooking, as the cheese will give the pastry a brown speckled appearance if it gets too hot. Cheese pastry as the covering for a vegetable pie served with cheese sauce makes an interesting dish for a change.

Cheese Fritters

4 tablespoons flour (self-raising)
2 eggs
4 tablespoons milk
1 oz. Cheddar cheese
Salt, pepper
Fat for frying

Put the flour in a bowl, break the eggs into the middle of it and mix well. Now add the milk and beat well until quite smooth, add seasoning to taste and the cheese cut into dice. Heat plenty of fat in a frying pan until it is smoking hot and drop in the batter, a tablespoon at a time. When golden brown on the underside turn over. When cooked, lift out with a spoon with holes in it so as to drain off all the fat. This quantity makes eight small fritters.

◆ ❖ ◆

The eggs, milk and cheese in this recipe provide the protein (body building material), the fat and flour provide carbohydrate (body energy and heat), so it has all the requirements of a main course. With a green vegetable, say spinach or a watercress salad, and with either fried or creamed potatoes, you have a well balanced meal. Garnish with parsley and baked or grilled tomatoes for an attractive, colourful dish. Cheese fritters are rich and definitely not for people with weak digestions.

Corn Fritters

1 tin sweetcorn
A pinch of sugar
Salt, pepper
1 oz. butter
A little parsley
3 tablespoons flour (self-raising)
1 egg
2 tablespoons milk
Fat for frying

Drain a tin of sweetcorn, keeping the juice. Place the corn in a pan with the sugar, seasoning, butter, one tablespoon flour and work over the heat until thick. If too dry add a little of the juice. Pour on to a plate to cool. Shape into rounds. Dip into batter and fry in hot fat. Drain on a paper and dish with fried parsley. To make the batter, put two tablespoons of flour into a bowl, break the egg into the middle and mix well; add the milk and beat until quite smooth. Corn fritters are usually served with Chicken Maryland (see page 80).

Fritters call for deep fat frying to get an even browning. Here are a few tips: the best frying medium is oil, which can be raised to a higher temperature than fat without burning, but clarified mutton or beef dripping and lard are also suitable. The fat should be quite still, bubbles indicate the presence of water in the fat; there should be a faint blue haze rising from the pan. The immersion of the food lowers the temperature of the fat and the surface will be covered with bubbles, when these have ceased, the fat has reheated and the food is cooking. For length of frying time, take into consideration the thickness of the mixture to be cooked, whether raw or reheated food, the texture (whether solid or of a light consistency), and vary the temperature of the fat accordingly. See that the fritters are evenly coated with batter – allow the surplus to drain off for a moment before frying.

Egg and Anchovy Savoury

1 egg
A large tomato
A few anchovy fillets
Bread
Butter

This is a good savoury or cocktail tit-bit. It looks quite professional and is very easy and economical to make. Hard-boil the egg. Plunge it into cold water. Shell and slice. Plunge the tomato into boiling water, skin and slice. Cut some rounds of bread about the diameter of the tomato. Fry them in butter on both sides. Allow them to cool. On each round of bread place a slice of tomato, then a slice of egg. Put a thin fillet of anchovy round the egg (if the anchovy fillets are too wide they must be cut in half lengthwise). Add a cross of anchovy on the top of each slice of egg. Serve cold.

The Scandinavian Smorgasbord or open sandwiches are variations on this theme, though the ingredients are usually served on thick buttered slices of rye bread. All sorts of food can be served this way, slices of smoked fish, cheese, cold meat or game, with chopped gherkins or chutney between layers of salad. You can in fact have every essential ingredient of a balanced meal: protein – the meat, fish, egg or cheese; carbohydrate – the bread, butter or mayonnaise dressing; and the vitamins and protective foods in the salad garnish. Smorgasbord look so attractive served on a large pretty china dish or wooden platter, and are an ideal garden lunch with beer, iced tea or coffee to drink.

Eggs in Aspic

4 eggs
1 or 2 tomatoes
A few slices of cucumber
4 slices of tongue or ham
Aspic
Sherry (optional)

Poach the eggs in a poacher, or failing that, poach very carefully and cut round with a biscuit cutter. Skin and slice the tomatoes and cucumber. Cut the tongue or ham round to fit under the eggs. Put each slice of meat with an egg on top of it in a shallow glass or entrée dish. Decorate the bottom of the dish with slices of tomato and cucumber cut into stars. Cover with aspic (this can be bought by the bottle and need not be made at home, though it is improved by the addition of a touch of sherry) and put to set in a refrigerator if you have one. If not, any cool place will do, but in that case leave overnight.

It is an original idea to serve a poached egg coated in aspic jelly. The usual way is to slice hard-boiled eggs and serve these between layers of jelly. In this recipe the aspic is served in the dish in which it sets, so the tricky business of unmoulding does not arise, but should you wish to serve individual jellies on lettuce leaves, remember that what you put at the bottom of the mould comes out on top, and be particularly careful to see that you have a good layer of fairly firm jelly before you put in the heavy things like egg and chopped meat, or they will sink to the bottom. To turn out a jelly, run the mould for an instant under the hot tap, loosen the edges with your fingers, give a sharp shake, and unmould on to your hand or straight on to the dish. Put a little clear aspic jelly into a deepish plate to set and chop it coarsely as a decoration. Aspics served in a nest of mustard and cress look very pretty.

Egg, Rice and Onion

2 tablespoons rice
2 medium onions
4 hard-boiled eggs
2 ozs. butter
A teaspoon chopped parsley
A little grated nutmeg

Put the rice into boiling water with the peeled onions. When the rice is cooked take out the onions and chop finely. Strain the rice and add the butter to it. Put back the onions and add the eggs, chopped, the parsley and the nutmeg to taste. Reheat and serve. This can be used as an entrée or a savoury and no-one will know of what it is made.

I have served this as a savoury on small squares of fried bread with a garnish of tomato, and it was very popular. When eggs were scarce I replaced them with grated cheese, added an additional tablespoon of rice, omitted the nutmeg and seasoned with a teaspoonful of sweet pickle. Served in a ring of creamed spinach with grilled rashers of bacon on top, it not only makes a delicious entrée, but provides a well balanced meal.

Gnocchi

Per Head:
1 oz. butter
2 tablespoons water
A heaped tablespoon flour
A little salt
1 egg
About ½ pint Mornay sauce (see page 137) for 4 people

Melt the butter in the water, sift in the flour, stirring all the while so that it does not go lumpy. Add the salt and egg, beat well until it comes away from the saucepan and leaves it quite clean. Boil some salted water in a large saucepan. Put the mixture in a piping bag, and as it comes out cut off pieces about half inch long so that they fall into the slowly boiling water. Poach for about 10 minutes, lift out into a hot heatproof dish with a spoon with holes in it, making sure that all the water drains off. Cover with the Mornay sauce and brown under the grill before serving. If you have no piping bag you can easily drop the mixture into the water from a small spoon, about half a teaspoonful at a time, keeping the pieces as round as possible.

◆ ❖ ◆

Until I saw this recipe I had always cooked gnocchi by making a stiff semolina paste and, when cool and stiff, baking, covered with grated cheese. However the method given above makes a much richer dish, if a little more trouble to prepare. The calorie content is very high, providing approximately 600 per portion, 3,500 being the recognised pre-war standard for the average man per day. It is rich in Vitamin A and contains calcium in the cheese and milk (Mornay sauce); if served as a savoury it can give nutritional substance to a light meal of the salad type, which would provide Vitamin C.

Marrow Bones

1 marrow bone per head
1 square of toast per head

Boil the marrow bones for at least an hour. Empty on to the hot toast by means of a pickle spoon (or failing that, a skewer) and serve immediately. It is essential that the marrow should be piping hot, so if you are not dining in the kitchen it is really advisable to serve the bones with a napkin round each and let each person help themselves. Be sure to see that there is pepper on the table, as marrow without salt and pepper is nauseating.

Marrow is a great delicacy. It consists of practically pure fat and must be served very hot or it is unpalatable and greasy. An alternative method of serving is to remove from the bones before cooking, chop and blanch (cover with cold water, add a little salt and bring to the boil for one moment), then turn into a basin of cold water and drain well, add herbs and seasoning, and pound together with a little hard-boiled egg yolk. Spread on toast or fried breadfingers (I prefer the latter), sprinkle with brown crumbs and warm through in a moderate oven. Marrow can be melted down and kept in sealed jars, it makes a good sandwich spread with watercress and seasoning.

Mushroom Flan

1 lb. mushrooms
¼ pint cream
Small piece of butter
Short pastry made with ¾ oz. fat and 1½ ozs. flour

Peel the mushrooms and cut into large slices, cook for 3-4 minutes in butter; bind with a little of the cream and let them get cold. Line a flan ring with the pastry, fill with the mushroom mixture; bake in a very hot oven for 15-20 minutes. Just before it is ready, pour the rest of the cream over the flan and serve immediately after you take it out of the oven.

◆ ❖ ◆

I suggest baking the flan case separately and adding the mushrooms once the pastry is cooked. You can be cooking them whilst the flan is in the oven. 1 lb. of mushrooms is a very generous allowance, and will make a flan providing four big portions. If you use the stalks as well, you can do very nicely with ½ lb. Increase the pastry quantities unless you can roll your paste very thin indeed. Garnish with paprika and sprigs of parsley. Delicious though they are, mushrooms have little food value and some people can't digest them, so before making mushrooms the 'pièce de résistance' of your dinner party be quite sure that all your guests can take it!

Mushroom Roly-Poly

4 ozs. suet
8 ozs. flour
1 teaspoon salt
1 lb. mushrooms
A piece of butter the size of an egg

Make the suet crust (see page 14), adding half the salt. Roll out into an oblong about a quarter inch thick. In the meantime, peel and stalk the mushrooms. Chop coarsely, add the rest of the salt and sauté in butter for about 5 minutes. Spread over the suet but be sure to leave about an inch all round; sprinkle with a little of the juice. Roll up, press the edges together, roll in a floured cloth. Tie up (it is best to use a single loop for tying so that it is easy to undo; cutting hot string is apt to scald the fingers). Leave plenty of room for the roly-poly to rise; put into a pan of boiling water and boil for about 2 hours. As this is a very solid dish it is really best to treat it as the principal course of a meal.

◆ ❖ ◆

Being a town dweller, and buying my mushrooms in ¼ lbs. as a special treat, I didn't think I would ever combine mushrooms with suet pudding, as to me it seemed rather like using my best lace-edged tea cloth for drying up, but when we were staying in the country recently and had mushrooms within a few minutes walking distance free for the gathering, I changed my point of view, and made this Roly-Poly for lunch on several occasions. I chopped some rashers of bacon and fried them with the mushrooms to give a little more substance to the dish one day, and another time mixed grated cheese in with the flour for the suet crust. This added the protein that was necessary for a main course. With the dish I served young peas, carrots and turnips cooked in a casserole, and cabbage boiled very quickly with hardly any water and dressed with melted butter.

Mushroom Turnovers

½ lb. mushrooms
A small slice of onion
2 tablespoons breadcrumbs
A scrap of butter
A tablespoon gravy
Salt, pepper
About 6 ozs. puff or short pastry

Cut the mushrooms small and put into a saucepan with the finely chopped onion, seasoning, a teacup of water, a tablespoon of gravy or meat extract and the breadcrumbs. Stew gently until the mushrooms have absorbed all the moisture. Turn on to a plate to cool. Cut the pastry into rounds the size of a teacup, brush the rims with milk; put a small teaspoon of mushroom into each and fold over. Bake in a quick oven for 15-20 minutes.

◆ ❖ ◆

Turnovers, whether they have a savoury or sweet filling, are often spoiled because the interior bursts out and burns itself away on the baking sheet, making a nasty mess to clear up. This can be avoided if you roll your pastry thin, and leave it in a cool place for about half an hour before cutting out. This allows for shrinkage which would otherwise occur during cooking. Do not let your filling be within half an inch of the edges, and see that you press them down firmly and then 'knock them up' well. 'Knocking up' means sharp taps with the back of a floured knife in a slightly lifting movement all around the edges of the pastry. It ensures a good seal and helps it to rise. Incidentally, beaten egg is a stronger seal than milk. Prick the turnovers once or twice so that the steam can escape (otherwise it will force its way out through the edges) and glaze with beaten egg. Always put pastry into a hot oven but reduce the heat slightly after 5 minutes. If your turnovers are browning too quickly cover with paper sprinkled lightly with water.

Noodles or Spaghetti with Tomato Sauce

2 handfuls of noodles per head
Scraps of cold meat, liver, sausage or bacon
Butter
Cheese
Salt, pepper

Boil a large pan of salted water; throw in the noodles or spaghetti and boil until soft (about 20 minutes). Drain and return to the saucepan with some butter, salt and pepper. Toss lightly and serve with tomato sauce (see page 141) to which you have added cubes of meat, liver, sausage or bacon. Serve grated cheese separately for those who like it.

This is a very 'filling' dish, but it doesn't have very much food value unless you are fairly generous with the pieces of meat and grated cheese. It could be dietetically improved by using fresh tomatoes skinned and sliced instead of tomato sauce, but is best used as an accompaniment to a meat course instead of potatoes, or in place of soup, with a salad to follow.

Oeufs à la Courgette

2 rashers streaky bacon
1 onion
½ small marrow
1 egg per head

Cut the bacon into strips and fry. As soon as the fat covers the frying pan add the peeled and diced marrow and the coarsely chopped onion. When cooked and nicely brown lift into a warmed entrée dish with a spoon with holes in it, so that all the fat remains in the frying pan. Now fry the eggs and dish up on the bed of mixed bacon and vegetables which you have been keeping hot in the oven.

I can recommend this, especially if you use a nice young marrow. It has protein and fat, and if you served fingers of fried bread with it you would have some additional carbohydrate, and the crispiness is a nice foil for the softness of the marrow. Personally, I like this very much served with a border of boiled rice, or if you feel you need some iron and vitamins, have creamed spinach. A note on frying bacon: flatten the rashers before cooking by scraping with a knife on a flat surface, and lightly dust with flour, this prevents them crinkling up to nothing. A pair of kitchen scissors is much the best medium for removing rinds, which should be kept for flavouring stews and soups.

Oeufs Mollets

Boil the eggs for 5 minutes. Plunge into cold water. Leave for a minute. Take out and crack each egg very gently then roll, pressing lightly on the egg with your hand until the shell is cracked all over. The shell should now come off easily. Serve with Mornay sauce (see page 137), sour cream sauce (see page 140), or cheese sauce (see page 131).

◆ ❖ ◆

A quickly prepared and nourishing dish which can be served to the most confirmed gourmet without a qualm. Present it on a bed of sweetcorn, carefully drained and warmed with a little melted butter, or surround with a border of peas or French beans, young carrots or grilled tomatoes. If you are using Mornay or cheese sauce, sprinkle a little cheese on the top and brown under the grill. Two eggs cooked this way provide 300 calories, a little more if you coat with the cheese sauce recipe, which is particularly rich. Eggs contain every food necessity except Vitamin C, and are rich in Vitamin A which protects against eye trouble.

Omelette

2 eggs per head
A small amount of butter
Salt, pepper

Omelettes are so easy to make that it is surprising how few good ones one gets in England. It is, however, essential to follow a few simple rules. Put a large frying-pan (and it must be a completely flat one) on the heat and warm up. Put in a very small piece of butter. When it has melted, brush it all over the pan with a pastry brush if you have one. If not, you must be sure that the pan is well covered by jiggling it about. Leave until very hot. In the meantime break the eggs into a bowl, season and break up with a fork. The eggs must not be whisked – just beat until the white and the yolk are fairly well mixed. Pour into the pan and shake all over. Keep on gathering the omelette to one side and letting the liquid part run over on to the bottom of the pan. When all the liquid is just not quite set roll over, and dish up with a palette knife. The result will be a French omelette with a golden brown exterior and a deliciously moist interior.

If you have several hungry people waiting to be fed with omelettes, it is much better to make one big omelette and serve it on a dish, cutting it up for each person, otherwise you'll have a staggered sort of meal, as of course you will insist that each omelette is eaten immediately it is cooked, and that will leave you eating yours while your guests look on with empty plates. I am sure you'll have plenty of ideas for fillings, which must be added hot to the centre of the omelette before rolling up. Three eggs are necessary per person if the omelette is to be a plain one and to provide the main course, but two are quite sufficient if you are adding a filling. A dessertspoon of cold water can be added to every two eggs if you want to make them go further, this makes the texture soft. Keep a special pan for omelettes and pancakes, don't wash it unless really necessary, wiping it round with kitchen paper after use is quite sufficient.

Scrambled Eggs

8 eggs
½ teacup milk if liked
A scrap of butter
Seasoning

Break the eggs into a basin and whisk with a fork until they are well broken but not completely mixed; add the milk and seasoning. Heat, the butter in a saucepan on a low heat, add the eggs and stir all the time until they are cooked.

Peas – Add the previously cooked peas just before serving.
Finnan Haddock – Flake some remains of cold haddock, mix with the eggs just before they have finished cooking; stir until the fish is heated through and serve.
Tomatoes – Skin three or four tomatoes, season and cook in butter until soft; break into small pieces and mix with the eggs just before serving
Brains – Blanche the brains, skin and chop up, cook in butter; pour the eggs on top and scramble in the usual way.
Mushrooms – Skin the mushrooms, chop up small and cook in butter; pour the eggs on top and scramble in the usual way.

◆ ❖ ◆

Is there anyone who can't make scrambled eggs? I doubt it, but there are quite a lot of really good cooks whose scrambled eggs are indifferent, and a surprising number of completely inexperienced ones – particularly men, I have found – who dish up the most succulent scrambles. Nothing could be simpler so long as you remember that an egg goes on cooking for several minutes after it leaves the heat, so, as soon as it begins to set take it off the heat, and dish it straight on to your toast or fried bread. This recipe just greases the pan with butter. Personally, for eight eggs, I should allow at least 2 ozs. of butter. If you want to make a large quantity, for a party, for instance, do it in a double saucepan. You can cheerfully forget about it while you are busy toasting because all the attention it needs is an occasional stir with a wooden spoon.

Spinach and Egg Jellies

1 lb. spinach
¼ pint beef stock
½ oz. powder gelatine
2 hard-boiled eggs
Salt, pepper

Wash spinach and remove coarser stalks. Boil slowly without adding any water; spinach makes its own water. Squeeze out well with a wooden spoon, strain off the juice and chop the vegetables coarsely. Boil up a quarter pint of spinach juice with the stock; melt gelatine in the mixture. Put the spinach in four ramekin cases, fill about three-quarters full, make a depression in the middle of each and place half an egg there. Fill up with the gelatine, etc., and put in a refrigerator or leave overnight to harden. When serving stand for an instant in hot water and then turn out.

Imagine these surrounded by rings of thinly sliced tomatoes and cucumber on crisp lettuce leaves. Lovely on a hot day and so slimming! Half an egg per person wouldn't provide sufficient protein for a main meal of course, because one egg provides only six grams of protein, and we need 70 grams daily to keep fit. For your information, cheese contains the highest amount of protein of any food – 7 grams per oz., meat and fish have six and five grams respectively – but as cheese has a high content of fat, you cannot eat as much of it at a sitting as you can of the other two. When you are setting a liquid with gelatine, it is advisable to test out your gelatine first, as different brands vary considerably. The usual amount is two ounces to three pints of liquid in summer, two ounces to three and a half pints in winter. If you have a refrigerator allow your jellies to cool before putting them inside, as steam from hot food taints the other contents.

Tomato Jelly

2 breakfast cups tomato juice
Pepper, celery salt
1 lump sugar
1½ dessertspoons powdered gelatine

Heat the tomato juice and add sugar, celery salt and pepper. Stir until the sugar has melted, then add the gelatine dissolved in one third breakfast cup water (preferably through a strainer). Stir well again and fill up four small ramekin cases. Turn out next day and serve with mayonnaise (see page 138) or Dutch sauce (see page 132) on a bed of lettuce.

◆ ❖ ◆

This is an excellent way of using your bottled tomatoes in winter; they will help out cold weather salads. Alternatively, if you reduce the gelatine slightly, you could serve tomato jelly as an iced soup in summer time. A little chopped mint could be added to the water used to dissolve the gelatine, but, if you do this, strain before adding to the tomato, as this gives a delicious tang to the jelly. Although of little nutritional value, jelly is of dietetic importance because it stimulates the digestive juices, and so helps digestion – that is why it is particularly suitable for invalid diets.

Torhonya

This is the Hungarian equivalent of Italian spaghetti or Chinese noodles.

To make:
1 lb. flour
1 egg
Salt

Mix the flour, salt and beaten-up egg with enough cold water to make a very stiff paste. Knead well. Grate on a coarse grater and dry the pieces, which are rather like breadcrumbs to look at, in a very slow oven until they are quite dry and hard. (This can be done in the sun, but not in England!) When done, shake through a colander as the coarser pieces take longer to cook than the little ones and they should be kept separate. Stored in covered jars the torhonya will keep for months.

To cook:
½ lb. torhonya
2 or 3 mushrooms
1 large onion

Peel and cut the mushrooms into small pieces. Chop the onion; fry both in some boiling lard until the onions are pale gold. Add torhonya and fry for a minute or two. Now add the boiling water and simmer slowly until all the water has disappeared and the torhonya is soft but not squashy. Add a drop more water if necessary. You can leave out the mushrooms and add bits of kidney or bacon, or anything else you fancy.

Any recipe suitable for macaroni or spaghetti could be used for Torhonya – it provides padding to a meal and each 4 ozs. used would put up the number of calories by 400. I have used Torhonya for a pudding by boiling it with milk and water until soft, mixing with eggs, sugar and dried fruit, and steaming until firm. It is very nice this way, especially if you serve it with an interesting sauce. When adding cereal to boiling water, sprinkle in slowly so that the bubbles hold the grains in suspension, and do not sink to the bottom, this will prevent burning.

Prunes in Bacon

16 prunes
8 rashers streaky bacon

Soak the prunes overnight. Stone and put one inside another. Wrap in a
rasher of bacon and grill immediately before serving. Can be served plain
or on a square of toast.

◆ ❖ ◆

*Here is a second cousin to Angels-on-Horseback, which is bacon
wrapped round an oyster. If you haven't tried bacon with something
sweet, I can assure you that you are in for a pleasant surprise. Fried
apple rings with the morning rashers are delicious and a nice change
from eggs or sausages – it is no different from pork and apple sauce after
all. Very rich food is made more digestible if eaten with something acid –
hence lamb and mint sauce, redcurrant jelly with mutton – or, to go down
the scale, vinegar with fish and chips! The best way to grill bacon rolls
is to thread them on a skewer which you can rest on the edges of the grill
pan, turning half way through the cooking so that the underside gets its
share of the heat.*

Sardine Fritters

Make in exactly the same way as cheese fritters (see page 33), only use about four sardines instead of the cheese. Remove the bones from the sardines before using them. Strain off all the oil and break each fish into two or three pieces.

◆ ❖ ◆

When you are coating something with batter, remember that the batter must be sufficiently thick and evenly applied to protect the contents from the boiling fat; when you are coating something moist like fish, it is advisable to dredge with flour just before immersing in the batter. If you hold your sardine on a skewer, you can dip it in and out of the batter without difficulty. To test fat for correct heat, drop a little of the batter into the pan, if it rises to the surface with a lot of bubbles it is right, if it sinks to the bottom it is too cool.

Cheese Wafers

16 Huntley & Palmer's plain wafers
Cheese, preferably gruyére
A little butter

Spread the wafers with butter. If it is cold weather, work the butter first until it is soft or you will break the wafers. Put a thin slice of cheese between two wafers like a sandwich and bake until the cheese has melted (a few minutes). Serve immediately.

◆ ❖ ◆

Just time to pop these in the oven while you are making coffee. I find it easier to mix butter with grated cheese and seasoning, not forgetting the mustard, and, if you have one to spare, moisten with egg yolk or cream. The secret of this is a very hot oven – 500° F. or 10-11 Regulo.

Grilled Cheese Biscuits

Butter some water biscuits. (Thin Captains or Romary's water biscuits are very good for this purpose.) Spread an even layer of grated cheese on each, add a sprinkling of pepper, grill until the cheese is melted and serve immediately. This only takes a minute or two under a hot grill.

Do you know that one ounce of hard cheese contains 120 calories, while the same weight of meat only provides 50! Cheese is, in fact, the most concentrated food there is – the actual constituents being ⅓ each of protein, fat and water. Hard cheeses are more easily digested than the softer variety. But cheese is not an easily digested food because of the high fat content. That is why we dilute the richness of cheese with a starchy material – bread and cheese, macaroni cheese, etc. Avoid overcooking as this makes it even more difficult for the tummy to cope with.

FISH

Cod Scallops

2 lbs. cod
1 tablespoon mixed herbs
4 bay leaves
2 tablespoons flour
2 tablespoons wine
Vinegar, salt, pepper
1 oz. butter

Put the cod in a saucepan. Cover with cold water and add herbs, bay leaves, vinegar and seasoning. Bring to the boil. Boil slowly for about 10 minutes. Remove from the heat. Melt the butter in a saucepan, add the flour and mix well. Gradually strain in the liquid in which the fish has been boiled. Remove the skin and bones from the cod, break the fish into small pieces. Return it to the sauce, heat up and serve in old scallop shells. You can cover with brown breadcrumbs and a few dabs of butter, and brown under a grill if you like.

♦ ❖ ♦

Fish is one of the chief sources of animal protein: it contains five grams per oz., compared with six grams in one oz. of meat or one egg. Fat fish like herrings, sprats and salmon have a high fat content also, making them even more nutritious. The old saying that fish is good for the brain is probably explained by the fact that fish provides an easily digested meal without giving that sleepy replete feeling that comes after suet pudding, and other solid foods containing a lot of carbohydrate. There is calcium in fish, especially in the little fellows – sprats, smelts and whitebait, and Vitamin A and B, though no Vitamin C. Any white fish can be scalloped in this way and the flavour varied with different sauces. Cheese sauce is a good variation. Instead of dotting with butter, melt a little in a frying pan, and toss the breadcrumbs in it, then fat is evenly distributed if you do this, and you will get an even browning.

Cold Fish and Lobster
or Prawn Mousse

1½ lbs. white fish	1 oz. butter
1 tablespoon mixed herbs	2 tablespoons flour
2 tablespoons vinegar	¼ pint milk or cream
2 bay leaves	¼ lb. lobster or prawns (tinned or fresh)
Salt, pepper	½ oz. powdered gelatine

Put the fish in a saucepan and cover with cold water. Add vinegar, bay-leaves, herbs and seasoning. Boil slowly for about 10 minutes. Remove the fish skin, debone and pound (or mash well with a fork if you have no pestle and mortar). In the meantime leave the fish stock on the heat to reduce. Remove the bay leaves. Melt the butter, add the flour, stirring all the time, then gradually add the boiling fish stock and lastly the milk or cream. This will make a stiff sauce. Now add the fish and the lobster or prawns broken into smallish pieces. Melt the gelatine in a little boiling water. Add to the mixture through a strainer. Mix all together well. Pour into a soufflé dish and leave if possible for 12 hours at least to set. Or put in a refrigerator.

◆ ❖ ◆

When boiling fish use a fish kettle, which has a perforated tray at the bottom so that you can lift the fish out easily, or use an ordinary saucepan and place a wire stand of some sort at the bottom, with strings attached to the sides to lift it out. For the sauce you will need about a pint of liquid, so reduce your stock to ¾ pint or just under. Rinse your mould in cold water before adding the mousse, if you want to turn it out. Serve on crisp lettuce leaves and garnish with prawn heads or lobster feelers, and sliced cucumber, or if you are using tinned fish, save a few pieces and arrange in a ring round the top.

Fillets de Sole au Vin Blanc

4 good sized fillets of Dover sole
½ small onion (chopped very fine)
Salt, pepper
A wineglass of cheap white wine
or ½ wineglass dry sherry and ½ wine glass lemon juice

Put all the ingredients in a flat buttered dish, cover with a greased paper and cook in the oven for about 15 minutes. If possible serve in the dish in which it has been cooked.

◆ ❖ ◆

Some of the finest cooking is the simplest. This dish comes into the gourmet class, yet nothing could be easier to prepare. Serve it with a green salad with a French Dressing, and plain boiled potatoes. Sprinkle a little chopped parsley on top of the fish. I prefer to use garlic instead of onion when baking, only a very little of course – a quarter of a clove, crushed and rubbed round the baking dish is quite sufficient.

Lobster au Gratin

About ½ pint of thick béchamel sauce (see page 129)
2 medium lobsters (or 2 half-pound tins of Cape spiny lobster)
A little butter
A very little lemon juice
A little chutney
Worcester sauce and seasoning to taste
Some brown breadcrumbs

Empty the shells and claws. Mix the sauce with chopped lobster meat, add all the other ingredients and return to the shells. Sprinkle with brown breadcrumbs, then with a little melted butter and bake in the oven for about 15 minutes. If you use tinned lobster, serve in scallop shells.

Grilled Scallops

2 scallops
About 1 oz. butter
Brown breadcrumbs

This is a suitable dish for two, as you cannot get more than two scallop shells under the average grill. Wash the shellfish and put back in the top half of the shell with a dab of butter on top. Grill under a slow grill for about 5 minutes. Turn over and cover with the breadcrumbs. Put plenty of butter in small dabs all over the crumbs and grill slowly for about 10 minutes (the exact time depends on the size of the scallops; these times are for average size). If you have an electric grill the best method is to turn it to hot, put the shells in the bottom of the grilling tin and stand that as far as possible from the heat. Alternatively, you can turn the grill to low and grill in the usual way, but this takes longer as the heat is very slow. Be sure that the crumbs are nicely soaked in butter. You can always add a few more little pieces if they look dry.

◆ ❖ ◆

This recipe can be recommended because it is simple and makes no mess. Most fish needs a certain amount of preparation, but scallops grilled in this way couldn't be easier. My tip about mixing the breadcrumbs with melted fat holds good here. Scallops are more easily digested than most shellfish, but they are inclined to be dry, so serve hot Dutch sauce (see page 132), or any other that you fancy, with them. Creamed potatoes and peas or young carrots would go well.

Fish Pie

1½ lbs. white fish	1 egg (optional)
½ pint béchamel sauce	About ½ lb. potatoes
3 or 4 tomatoes	About ½ teacup milk
Salt, pepper	A small lump of butter
1 tablespoon vinegar	1 dessertspoon mixed herbs

Any cheap white fish, preferably filleted (otherwise you have to bone it). Put the fish, vinegar, herbs, salt and pepper in a saucepan. Cover with cold water. Bring to the boil and simmer for 5-10 minutes until the fish is cooked, when the skin will easily come away from the flesh. Drain off the water, remove the skin (and bones if any). Hard-boil the egg. Mix the fish with the béchamel sauce (see page 129). I always use a soufflé dish for fish pie as it makes it look much more elegant, but a pie dish does just as well. Put a layer of the fish mixture in the bottom of the dish; now add a layer of sliced and skinned tomato, now a layer of fish, now a layer of sliced egg or another layer of tomato. Finish with a layer of fish. Top this with a thin layer of mashed potato, which should be well dried and mixed with the butter and milk before adding. Place a few little pieces of butter on the top and bake on the top of a medium oven for about half an hour, until nicely browned.

The essentials of this excellent but much maligned dish are that the inside should be creamy and the potato layer thin and buttery. About an inch of dry white fish at the bottom of a dish topped with a lot of dry mashed potato is quite wrong and most unnecessary. Fish pie can be made beforehand and heated up.

Any dish that can be prepared in advance should have a double star in your recipe book, because so often in these busy days, wear and tear on the cook produces a nervy atmosphere at the dinner table, which quite literally can upset the digestion and make the most delicious food unappetising. It is far better to sit down promptly to bread and cheese with a smile than to keep the family waiting for an elaborate meal which you have had to cook against time. If cooking is planned with method, and you have a few tins ready for emergencies, you will soon get that precious reputation of being not only a good caterer, but a good tempered one as well.

Haddock Savoy

1 finnan haddock
A tumbler of milk
A little cream
2½ozs. butter
1 tablespoon flour
About a dozen asparagus tips
1 or 2 tomatoes
Pepper
1 egg

Poach the haddock in milk to which some cream has been added. When the fish is cooked remove it from the liquid, take off the grey skin and put it in the oven to keep warm. Melt 2 ozs. butter, add the flour and stir well, then gradually add the milk in which the fish has been cooked, stirring all the time so that there are no lumps. Let the mixture boil, then remove from the heat and add the yolk of an egg. Mix well and put back on the stove for a minute or so but do not let it boil. Meanwhile cook the asparagus tips. Skin the tomatoes, slice them and fry in the remains of the butter for a few minutes. Place the asparagus tips and the tomato decoratively round the haddock. Cover with the sauce and serve.

When cooking asparagus tie the stalks together with a piece of string to prevent them breaking. Simmer gently or the heads will come off. When done, the middle of the stalk should be soft enough to eat. Save the water and the parts you are not using and make into soup. Boil hard in a covered pan for some time and you will have a well-flavoured stock that can be added to a cream sauce and makes a delicious soup. Tomatoes and asparagus are lovely together, and Haddock Savoy is a real party recipe; but for something less extravagant, a few mushroom stalks chopped and poached with the fish are delicious in place of the asparagus; or chopped hard-boiled egg added to the sauce is another excellent variation.

Kedgeree

Take a handful of rice per head and boil it (see page 12). Mix it with the same quantity of flaked boiled fish. The nicest kedgeree is made with finnan haddock, but salmon (even tinned) is very good. Less good of course, are any of the white fishes such as cod or hake. Add half a boiled egg per head, chopped. Put in a saucepan with plenty of butter and stir well until the butter is all melted and the mixture is hot. If you do not use finnan haddock, season with salt, and whatever fish you use season with pepper.

◆ ❖ ◆

This is one of my favourite breakfast dishes, and I agree that smoked haddock is by far the nicest fish to use. It is a most satisfactory way of using up cold fish, because any leftovers can be mixed in with the rice. Kedgeree should be quite moist, buttery and very hot. Be careful not to mash the rice: each grain should be separate. I find the easiest way to heat it up is in a double saucepan or in a basin in a pan of boiling water, and I add my egg as a garnish otherwise it seems to get lost among the rice. Add plenty of pepper and sprinkle the dish with chopped parsley and paprika. The calorie content is high, providing building fuel and energy food. It also contains Vitamin A and a certain amount of B and C if you are generous with the parsley.

Lobster Scallops

2 half-pound tins Cape spiny lobster
2½ ozs. butter
2 tablespoons flour
A spoonful or two of cream (optional)
4 tablespoons cooking sherry

1 egg
3 or 4 potatoes
A little milk
Salt, pepper

This dish can, of course, be made with fresh lobster, but the tinned variety is very good and much cheaper. Make two holes in each of the tins and drain off all the liquid into a bowl or jug. Now open the tins and mash up all the meat with a fork. Put 2 ozs. of butter in a saucepan, add the flour, mix well and add the lobster liquid gradually, stirring all the time until it boils. Now mix in the sherry, seasoning and the cream if you can spare any. Lastly add the well beaten egg, but do not let it boil once the egg is added. In the meantime cook and mash the potatoes, add the milk, ½ oz. of butter, salt and pepper. Mix the fish with the sauce, heat up, put into four scallop shells, decorate with a ring of potato (this looks best put through a piping bag, but can be perfectly well done with a small spoon) and put under the grill or in the oven for a few minutes before serving. Can be made in advance and reheated, but care must be taken not to let it boil.

You have the basis here for a Lobster Patty filling or a Lobster Croquette mixture. Amazing what a dash of sherry or white wine can do! – never be without a bottle in your kitchen cupboard, don't be heavy handed or you'll ruin the dish. Keep a little of the egg yolk back and brush over the potato, it will give it a nice brown glaze. To make washing up easier, grease your scallop shells. While we are on the subject of shellfish, just a word about their nutritional value – appetising certainly, and excellent to ring the changes in the diet occasionally, but they have little or no food value and as a class are generally indigestible, lobster particularly, because of the coarse fibres of the flesh. Most shellfish have an inedible part, which must be carefully removed.

Pickled Fish

Enough white fish for four
2 onions
Small piece butter, lard or margarine
½ pint water
2 tablespoons curry powder
½ pint vinegar

Boil or steam the fish. When cooked, skin it and let it get cold. Cut the onions into rings and fry a golden brown. Now add the vinegar, water and curry powder and simmer until the onion is soft (45 minutes to 1 hour). Pour over the fish, covering it well. Leave for 24 hours before serving.

With a little care, any fish on the insipid side can be made much more delectable by careful flavouring. This recipe gives you a simple dish on the marinade principle. That is soaking food in some sort of flavoured liquid. Uninteresting white fish can also be much improved by boiling in Court Bouillon, which is a particularly well-seasoned fish stock made from fish trimmings, herbs, vegetables, white wine or vinegar and water (1 gill to 2 qts.). This bouillon can be used a second time if kept in a cool place between whiles.

Shredded Fish

2 lbs. white fish
1 piece of butter the size of an egg
Salt, pepper
1½ tablespoons flour
3 tablespoons sherry
2 dessertspoons mustard
½ pint milk

Cook the fish, skin, bone and flake. Make a white sauce, add the sherry and the mustard mixed with a little water. Stir in the fish, season and serve hot or cold. If served cold, it is nice on a bed of lettuce and decorated with beetroot and hard-boiled egg.

Here you have the same cooking principle as for Lobster Scallops, the only difference being in the serving, and the addition of the mustard to the sauce in place of the egg. It might be called Fricassee of Fish if served hot, or Fish Mayonnaise if it is chilled. Personally I think a cold fish salad is delicious and makes an excellent change from meat salads. Care should be taken to dish it neatly, however, or it can look anything but appetising. I serve mine in a shallow dish lined with nice looking lettuce leaves and trim the top with sliced cucumber and tomato (not beetroot because the colour will run out and spoil your mayonnaise).

Soused Herrings
or Mackerel

6 herrings
1 onion
3 or 4 bay leaves
A breakfast cup of vinegar
Salt, pepper

Cut the heads and tails off the herrings and split them down the centre of the back. Remove the bones. Cut the onion into slices and put a slice into each herring. Roll up the fish and pack into a casserole. Add the bay leaves, vinegar, a breakfast cup of water, salt and pepper. Bake in a slow oven for about 1½ hours. This dish can be equally well made with mackerel. Made with either fish it keeps for several days.

A little pickling spice can be sprinkled between the fish if you are fond of a spicy flavour, bruised root ginger, parsley stalks, or thick slices of cucumber or gherkin are sometimes added to the casserole. Soused herrings are good for Hors D'oeuvres, or as the protein part of a salad.

Cold Turbot Tartlets

Allow one large tartlet made with short pastry per head. Fill with cold boiled turbot; mask with mayonnaise (see page 138). Decorate with sieved hard-boiled yolk and white of egg alternately round the edge, and cucumber, beetroot and/or tomato in the middle.

It is a good idea to make a little extra pastry when you are at it and keep a few tartlet cases in reserve. Kept in a tin they will remain fresh for several days and are very useful when you want a meal in a hurry. Any tinned or cold fish can be served on the lines of the recipe. Flaked cold kippers (a nuisance to bone, I know, but if you do them warm it is not so difficult) in a cream-enriched white sauce, served in tartlet cases with the egg garnish are awfully good for supper, with a green salad and new potatoes.

Steamed Fish

This is a dish for invalids. It is quickly done and easily digested. Put two fillets of plaice, lemon or Dover sole on a large plate, season, add about two tablespoons of milk and a dab of butter. Put another plate on top and steam over a large pan of boiling water for about 10 minutes.

◆ ❖ ◆

This is by far the best way of steaming fish because, not only is it quick and simple, but none of the valuable solvents are wasted. The fish cooks in its own steam and the resulting liquid should be poured over it or used for making a sauce. According to the size and thickness of the fish, cook for 10-20 minutes; you can put your plates over the saucepan in which the potatoes are cooking, so saving fuel and space on the stove.

Fish hasn't much flavour by itself, and it needs something to make it appetising and stimulating. A dust of nutmeg or a few herbs can make all the difference, and if you are feeding an invalid, take pity on the poor soul and try and make his steamed fish as interesting as possible, even if it is only in appearance. Chopped parsley or savoury butter does a lot to glamorise a steamed fillet – which should be served piping hot, it is impossible to tempt a poor appetite with tepid food.

Finnan Haddock in Milk

A medium size haddock
A breakfast cup of milk
Pepper
A piece of butter the size of an egg

Put all the ingredients in a flat uncovered dish and cook in the oven for about 15-20 minutes. Baste occasionally.

Here's something that most men go for in a big way! Good for high tea with a poached egg on top, and lots of bread and butter. A 2 lb. haddock cooked like this would provide about 1,450 calories, and 160 grams of protein. Split among four people it supplies a very nourishing meal. Any smoked fish is nice poached in milk. Remember to serve some of the juice with the fish and add a knob of butter and some paprika on top before taking it to table.

Soft Roes in Bacon

8 roes
8 rashers streaky bacon
Cayenne pepper

Roll each roe in a piece of bacon. Grill about 5 minutes each side. Add a touch of cayenne and serve on small rounds of brown bread or toast.

Herring roes are the most nourishing, they are rich in vitamins and easily digestible – especially suitable for anyone who wants 'feeding up' or suffers from anaemia. They are good for children too, though perhaps the method suggested in this recipe would be a little on the rich side for young digestions. Wash the roes before cooking by putting in a colander in cold water for a minute or two, then shake once or twice and stand aside to drain. Dry them gently and coat lightly in flour, they are now ready for cooking so proceed with the directions given.

Soft Roes with Tomato Sauce

Fry 1 lb. of soft roes about 5 minutes each side in butter; add salt and pepper, and serve immediately on squares of brown bread (buttered) or toast. The Tomato Sauce (see page 141) is nicest served separately.

◆ ❖ ◆

As roes are so rich in vitamins – particularly Vitamin A – they can be given to children after they have reached about 18 months, in place of cod liver oil. This is a simple way to serve them: wash the roes and cook gently in milk for about 10 minutes, and then mash them up with potatoes (baked for extra nourishment, as the Vitamin C does not escape in a dry heat) or with creamed spinach or any other vegetable. When introducing roes to a baby's diet, begin gradually, with a teaspoonful to start with, increasing up to a tablespoon. Incidentally, for grown-ups roes fried in butter and served on toast spread with anchovy paste are very good, if you don't want to bother with tomato sauce.

MEAT, GAME
AND POULTRY

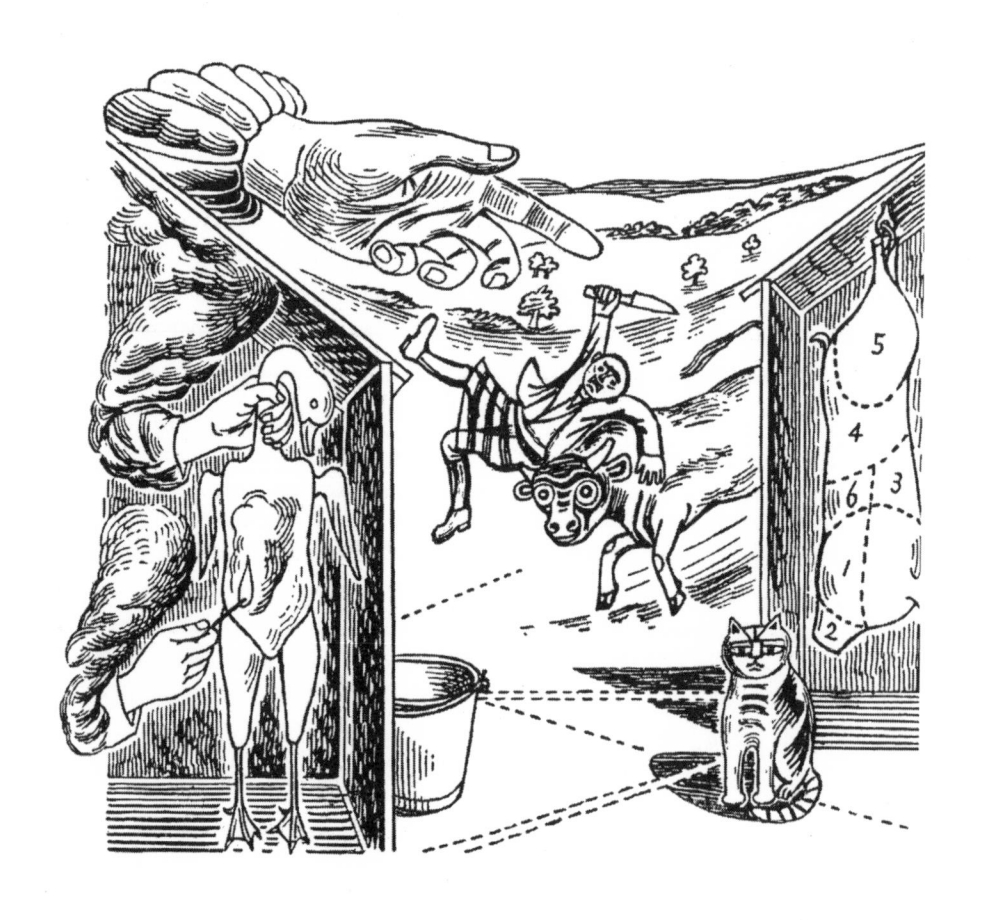

Backhendl

This is the Viennese equivalent to our Sunday joint. Clean and cut a spring chicken (the smaller the better) into four or six portions. Remove the skin and salt lightly. Dip first into flour, then in slightly beaten egg and lastly into breadcrumbs. The breadcrumbs should be very fine and made from white bread sliced and well dried in the oven. Be careful to see that the pieces of chicken are well coated all round. Fry in a deep saucepan in lots of fat (preferably lard or oil). Put on blotting paper to drain surplus fat and serve hot with salad and, when possible, new potatoes.

◆ ❖ ◆

I have never been to Vienna and have never eaten Backhendl but I love Escallop of Veal, and Backhendl is chicken cooked in the same way. I think anything that is covered in egg and crumbs should hold no surprises in the way of bones or other inedible portions inside the brown crust, so I suggest boning your chicken. This is quite easy if you have a small sharp pointed knife. Draw the sinews and break off the legs at the knee joints, and dislocate the wing and thigh bones by giving them a sharp backward twist. Slit the flesh from the back of the neck to the tail, and, keeping the point of the knife close to the bones, ease off the flesh as far as the leg and wing sockets, now turn over and repeat from the breast downwards, you should now be able to remove the carcass without difficulty. It is easier to bone a bird before it has been drawn.

Beef and Barley Stew

2 lbs. stewing steak
Salt, pepper
1 dessertspoon celery salt
2 lbs. carrots
2 onions
A little dripping or lard
1 tablespoon mixed herbs
3 handsful pearl barley
2 bay leaves

Remove all the gristle from the meat and cut it into chunks. Season. Cut the carrots and onions into rings. Put the fat in the bottom of a casserole on a low heat. When boiling, add the onions and herbs and stir frequently. When golden brown, remove and fry the meat on both sides. You may not be able to get it all in at once but this does not matter. Return to the casserole with the onions; cover with boiling water, add the bay leaves, carrots and barley, and stew for about 2 hours.

*When stewing meat, it is good to bear in mind the old adage –
'a stew boiling is a stew spoiling'. The cheaper cuts of meat have all the
nourishment of the more expensive parts and can be made just as tender
if they are subjected to slow gentle cooking never above simmering point.
Rapid boiling hardens the fibres and makes the meat shrink. Very tough
meat can be softened before cooking by dipping into vinegar for a few
minutes; the frying process should be omitted in this case and the liquid
used for cooking should be cold when the meat is put into it. When cutting
up meat for stews cut across the fibres, never down them.*

Braised Partridge

3 or 4 shallots or small onions	A small cabbage
A lump of fat	A bouquet of thyme, bay leaf, parsley
2 old partridges	(tied together)
2 carrots	Salt, pepper
6 rashers streaky bacon	

Fry the shallots or onions in the bottom of a casserole for a few minutes (if you can't get small ones you must slice large ones) and remove. Cut the partridges in two and fry on both sides. Remove. Cut the bacon into small pieces, lay in the bottom of the dish with the finely sliced carrot, the herbs and the onion. Lay the birds on this bed, add seasoning and about a teacup of stock or water. Cover and cook for about an hour – either on top or in the oven. Parboil the cabbage and add to the birds. Cook a further half-hour. Remove the herbs and serve in the casserole which has been used for cooking. If you cannot get sprigs of herbs, a teaspoonful of dried mixed herbs and a bay leaf will do instead. In this case you cannot remove the herbs before serving but be sure to remove the bay leaf which is completely inedible!

♦ ❖ ♦

Braising is a combination of stewing and baking, and the food cooked this way has a particularly rich flavour because the loss from evaporation is so slight. The foundation bed of vegetables and bacon imparts additional savouriness to the meat. Theoretically, the first two-thirds of the cooking should be done on the top of the stove over a gentle heat with frequent basting, and the last 20 minutes should be in a moderate oven. However, it is much simpler to do the whole thing in the oven, and if you cover the dish with buttered paper before putting on the lid, basting is unnecessary. Although it saves time and, if you have nice ovenware, the dish looks quite attractive served from the casserole, I think you will find it easier to serve if it is arranged on a large dish. Any liquid should be reduced until syrupy, and poured over the meat to glaze it. Garnish with bacon rolls and chopped parsley and, if you wish, forcemeat balls.

Braised Pork Chops

1½ lbs. pork chops
¾-1 pint milk (hot)
2 tablespoons butter
2 sliced onions
2 tablespoons flour
Salt, pepper

Wipe the chops with a damp cloth, sprinkle them with salt and pepper, dredge with flour. Sauté in hot butter until both sides are nicely browned. Pour over the milk and put in the onion. Simmer for 45 minutes to 1 hour.

If you are not careful you will have a rich layer of grease on the top of your gravy unless your chops are exceptionally lean, so I suggest you trim off some of the fat (you can render this down in the oven for dripping), and skim the sauce once or twice during cooking and again before serving. I suggest a casserole in a moderate oven but see that it remains at an even temperature or the milk will boil over. Counteract the richness with something tart – apple or tomato sauce, or chutney. Having such a high proportion of fat, pork is rich in calories – one 8 oz. chop providing 800. It also contains the nerve Vitamin B, and some calcium.

Brawn

Half a pig's head
1 lb. of lean beef (optional)
6 peppercorns
1 teaspoon pickling spice
2 teaspoons mixed herbs
9 cloves
1 very small onion

If you can get the butcher to pickle the pig's head for ten days, do so, otherwise rub salt well in and leave for 24 hours, but this is not so good. The butcher will chop the head and remove the eyes. Wash the head and put it into a saucepan with the chopped-up beef and cover with lukewarm water. Put all the rest of the ingredients in a little muslin bag, tie up, and put in the water; put the lid on and simmer for 3 or 4 hours (until the meat comes right off the bones). Remove the muslin bag. Take out the beef and pig's head. Remove all bones, chop all the meat up together, leaving out the ear. Fill two medium size pudding basins or moulds with the meat; now add the liquid, mixing well with a fork so that it penetrates to the bottom of the moulds. Leave for at least 24 hours in winter or 48 hours in summer. Turn out when set. This recipe is enough for about eight people. Serve with mustard, brown sugar and vinegar, mixed according to taste, on each individual's plate.

◆ ❖ ◆

Here is a recipe for a pickling mixture which is excellent for pork, so, if you want to have a really good brawn, and the butcher won't oblige, put your pig's head (rubbed with salt as directed) and the beef into this brine, and turn daily for five or six days: 3 qts. of water, 1 lb. of salt, 1 oz. salt-petre, 1 lb. sugar: boil all together for 20 minutes and skim well. Pour into an earthenware pan and leave until cold, when it will be ready for the meat. The sugar can be omitted but it greatly improves the flavour of the meat. This pickle can be used again if more salt is added and it is boiled up and carefully skimmed.

Chicken Maryland

1 young chicken
1 lb. lard
Salt, pepper
A little flour
1 pint milk

Joint the chicken. Melt the lard in a very large frying pan. Dredge the bird plentifully with flour, salt and pepper then fry. Pour off some of the grease and add the milk to make a cream sauce. If the sauce is too thin, thicken by dredging in a little more flour.

If you prefer it you can bone your chicken before frying, it is more trouble but it so much easier to eat that I think it is worth it. The traditional accompaniments to Chicken Maryland are fried bananas (split down the centre and gently sautéed in butter) and sweetcorn. For especially succulent chicken, marinate the joints in olive oil for half an hour before frying. Your sauce should be very rich and creamy, a beaten egg yolk and a little cream will do the trick, and I like a dash of lemon juice added at the last moment.

Chicken Pie

1 small onion
A small piece of butter or some bacon fat
4-6 rashers streaky bacon
1 egg
1 small chicken
Rough puff pastry made with 2 ozs. fat and 3 ozs. self-raising flour
A little pepper

Peel and chop the onion. Cut the bacon into small pieces. Hard-boil and peel the egg (see page 19). Skin and joint the chicken. Fry the onion in a large saucepan until just coloured then fry the pieces of chicken for a minute or so on each side. Add a little boiling water and cook about 10 minutes. Now add the bacon and cook until the chicken is almost done. Pack into a pie dish with the egg cut into slices, pour over the chicken stock until the dish is nearly full. Put a ribbon of pastry round the edge of the dish before you cover with the pastry. Leave a little hole in the middle for the steam to escape. Cook a little knob separately to fill the hole and decorate round it with a few pastry leaves. Paint over with beaten egg. Bake in a moderate oven until the pastry is a golden brown, fill the little hole and serve hot or cold.

◆ ❖ ◆

If you are not sure of the tenderness of your bird, it is a good plan to steam it for a short time before jointing. Incidentally, this is a good trick if you want to roast or fry a chicken that is past its prime; half to three-quarters of an hour in a steamer will do wonders to the oldest hen, which can then be roasted for the same time with excellent results. A rasher or two of bacon on the breast during roasting will give it more flavour. Quite often when baking a pie, a lot of liquid evaporates, so use a funnel to add stock – a good gelatinous stock if you want to serve your pie cold, so that it will set into a stiff jelly – or scalded cream, for a hot pie. Sherry added to the stock will improve the flavour.

Cold Oxtail Jelly

1 oxtail
3 or 4 peeled tomatoes
Salt, pepper and celery salt
A good pinch of mixed herbs
2 bay-leaves

Wash the oxtail, cut into joints and season. Put into a deep casserole with all the other ingredients, cover with water and bring to the boil slowly. Simmer for several hours (this depends on the size of the oxtail) until the gristle at the end of each bone comes away in a small round slab. There is no need to finish cooking in one go, and it can be cooked on the top of the stove or in the oven, so it is quite economical with fuel. When cooked, remove all the bone and gristle from the meat, shred and put into a large mould or basin. Add the liquid from which you have removed the bay leaves. Leave overnight to set. Before serving take off the fat which will cover the top of the jelly, stand the basin or mould in hot water for an instant, then turn out on to a bed of lettuce.

Here you have a very economical and nutritious dish which is easy to prepare and slips down nicely on hot days, with salad. I add a few green peas to the mould when pouring on the stock because I like colour interest in my dishes. Oxtails are often dirty, and may need soaking to remove the dried blood, a little salt rubbed on the tail will help.

Corned Beef Hash

1 lb. potatoes
A little dripping or lard
1 lb. corned beef

Peel and boil the potatoes. Break up the beef into small pieces and put in a frying pan on a low heat. When the fat begins to melt add the potatoes, also broken into small pieces. Cook, stirring frequently, until the mixture is well mixed. Add a little fat if it is too dry. This can be served with fried eggs on the top, but I think it is nicer plain.

◆ ❖ ◆

I wonder how many times that odd tin of corned beef has steered you through an emergency. I can remember many occasions when my war-time larder could boast of little else, and all the ingenuity available was used to disguise it in a hundred and one different dresses, but we all agreed that you couldn't beat Hash! Though we liked chopped onion added with the potatoes; nicest with lightly cooked brussels sprouts arranged around and grilled tomatoes as a garnish. Plenty of calories are in the amounts given, four portions would each provide about 330, so I suggest a light sweet with a fruit base to make up Vitamin C and mineral requirements.

Fried Young Rabbit

3 ozs. lard
2 very young rabbits
About 3 heaped tablespoons flour
Salt, pepper, nutmeg
½ pint milk

Put the lard in a large frying pan on the heat. Dredge the jointed rabbits with seasoned flour and fry on both sides until golden brown (about 7 minutes on each side). Remove from the pan and keep warm. Dredge a little more flour into the pan, grate in a touch of nutmeg, add salt, pepper and the milk. Cook for a minute or two, stirring all the time and serve seperately in a sauceboat. This dish must be made with very young rabbits or it will be tough and dry.

Here is a poor relation of Chicken Maryland. If you marinate the joints as I suggested, the rabbit will be nicer and more nutritious too. Wild rabbits are far better flavoured than tame ones, although the latter have whiter, more delicate flesh and are much bigger. Always choose a young rabbit which should have been killed not more than two days before cooking. The jaw of a young rabbit should snap easily, and there should be a little nut in the joint of the paw, this disappears as the animal gets older. Because of the dryness of the flesh, bacon usually accompanies rabbit dishes.

Gammon Rashers with Mustard

2 gammon rashers
2 tablespoons dry mustard
2 tablespoons brown sugar
2 breakfast-cups of milk

Rub a mixture of the sugar and mustard into both sides of the rashers. Put in a flat dish. Add the milk and bake for about an hour. The milk should only reach the top of the gammon and not cover it.

◆ ❖ ◆

This is a good way to cook gammon which you think may be on the leathery side, because the coating of sugar and mustard will protect the fibres from hardening. Serve in the baking dish if it is a nice one, or dish with the sauce poured around. Have a fairly gentle oven or the milk will boil away. Broad beans tossed in butter and sprinkled with chopped parsley and boiled potatoes would be nice with this. There is Vitamin B1, the nerve protector, in gammon. In fact 4 ozs. (a good sized rasher) provides more than half the daily requirement of this Vitamin.

Grilled Gammon Rashers with Cider Sauce

2 gammon rashers

The rashers should be about half an inch thick, and should be grilled on both sides until lightly brown. Serve the sauce separately.

For the cider sauce:
1 pint cider (as dry as possible)
¼ lb. brown sugar
1 clove
Salt
Pepper
A bay leaf

Simmer all the ingredients in a saucepan until they thicken. Strain and reheat. Can be made beforehand.

Cider imparts a delicious tang to gammon. A baked ham, that is basted with cider, is something to be remembered too, so when I first read this recipe I couldn't resist trying it at once. A good draught cider is the best for cooking purposes or can be substituted for wine in recipes; bottled cider is too aerated. If your rashers are on the lean side, it is wise to brush your gammon and rub the grid, on which you are going to grill it, with bacon or ham fat, this will prevent hardening; turn once or twice and don't overcook.

Kidneys with Sherry and Rice

8 sheep's kidneys
A little flour
A piece of butter the size of a walnut
Pepper, salt
4 handsful of rice
2 tablespoons sherry

Skin the kidneys. Chop them. Dredge with flour. Melt the butter, add the kidneys and cook for about 5 minutes, add the sherry and seasoning and cook for another minute or two. Stir well so that the mixture does not catch. Keep warm, or cook in advance and heat up when required. Serve with boiled rice separately (see page 12) or serve the rice in a ring with the kidneys in the middle.

◆ ❖ ◆

Kidneys harden easily so fry them gently. The flour coating will protect their tender outer surface. Offal of any sort should be washed very carefully with a little salt. Coring kidneys is a fiddly business but most essential. A sharp, well pointed knife is necessary for this. I wouldn't let the mixture boil after adding the sherry, or you'll spoil the flavour, so shake the pan about to thoroughly mix, without allowing it to remain stationary on the heat.

Liver with Apple

1½ lbs. liver
½ lb. cooking apples
2 small onions
Salt, pepper
A dessertspoon mixed herbs
½ handful sultanas
A little butter or lard

Cut the liver into small slices. Season. Peel and core the apples and make into a thick purée. Chop the onions and fry in a little fat, add the herbs. Now add the purée, sultanas, salt and pepper and cook all together a few minutes. Melt some fat in the bottom of a casserole. Put in the liver and fry on each side for about 5 minutes. Put the apple mixture on top. Heat thoroughly and serve. While English calves' liver is the best for all liver dishes, this method disguises bullocks' liver or foreign calves'. Serve this dish with rashers of crisp streaky bacon.

◆ ❖ ◆

Liver contains an immense quantity of Vitamin A which is essential for human life. It is most important that children have sufficient quantities of this vitamin. Each day the body needs approximately 5,000 International Units. 1 oz. of liver contains 7,000 units as well as a lot of iron and calcium, so put liver high on your butcher's list if you want plenty of nourishment in your menus. Wash the liver carefully in salted water before use and remove the skin and pipes before cooking.

Macedoine au Tomates

½ lb. ham, tongue or remains of cold meat
¼ lb. cooked macaroni
Parsley
2 eggs (1 hard-boiled)
5 tomatoes
1 big onion
½ pint béchamel sauce (see page 129)
Some sippets of fried bread

Mince the meat and parsley; chop the macaroni and mix together with the raw egg. Grease a bowl and put in the mixture. Cook for half an hour 'au bain Marie' (i.e., the bowl put in a saucepan filled with water to the rim of the basin). Cook the onion and tomatoes and put through a sieve. Add to the béchamel sauce which must be thick. Turn the meat mixture on to a dish; pour the sauce over and decorate with the yellow and white of the egg which you have previously put through a sieve or chopped, and sippets of fried bread.

Reheated meat loses some of its nourishment, so if you want to serve this as a main course you should incorporate some additional protein in the way of cheese or egg. This dish is savoury and nutritious, having calcium and Vitamin C in the tomatoes and additional calories from the fried bread and macaroni, and would make a good supper dish or a light lunch. Cook your onions (which should be chopped to save time) and the tomatoes with a little fat and just a drop of water. Second class tomatoes are quite suitable for this recipe.

Paprika Chicken

2 onions
A medium sized chicken
2 tablespoons fat
3 tablespoons sour cream
About a tablespoon Hungarian paprika ·
Salt

Chop the onions fine and fry in the fat until golden brown. Add the paprika, joint the chicken and fry it on both sides until it is red in colour. Now add enough cold water to cover the meat, and salt to taste. Simmer very gently until the chicken is cooked and the gravy fairly thick. If necessary add more water. Before serving add the sour cream but do not boil after the cream has been added. One must have real paprika for this dish, otherwise it tastes ersatz, and the main thing is to get the sauce the right consistency – not too thin. Some people add a small spoonful of flour to the cream before adding it to the sauce, as this keeps it from becoming watery.

This dish should be tried out on the family before serving at a dinner party. The sour cream may at first sight put you off but I can assure you it is delicious, and the chicken looks very attractive in its creamy red sauce. The secret of stewing chicken so that it is really tender without being overcooked and stringy, lies in using a very gentle heat. Simmering point is between 160°-180° F.; the liquid should be almost still with just an occasional bubble rising to the surface. If you find difficulty in getting a low enough heat, use an asbestos mat or a piece of metal over your lowest burner, in this way you can cook several pots over the same flame.

Poulette au Vinaigre

A spring chicken
A tablespoon wine or tarragon vinegar
1 egg
Salt, pepper

Joint and skin the chicken, put in a saucepan with about an inch of water and the vinegar. Simmer until cooked – about twenty minutes. Add the seasoning and the well-beaten egg. Return to the heat and stir continually until the sauce thickens. Do not let it boil or it will curdle.

◆ ❖ ◆

There are so many delicious ways of cooking chicken in this book that I find it difficult to advise on them all. This particular recipe has the advantage of being quick to prepare, but you must have a tender chicken. A bird is considered a 'chicken' until it is nine months old. The quickest way to tell whether you have a youngster is to feel the end of the breastbone: if it is soft and gristly, you are on to a good thing. Beware of hairy-legged fowls, they are usually old and tough. The white skinned bird is considered best for boiling, those with yellow skins and black legs more suitable for roasting and frying.

Rabbit and Cucumber

1 cucumber
½ pint vinegar
1 bay leaf
1 rabbit
A little fat
A tablespoon flour
A little cream (optional)
Salt, pepper
½ teacup milk

Peel and cut the cucumber into slices. Lay it in the vinegar with the bay leaf for about 2 hours then strain out the vinegar. Melt the fat in a casserole, fry the rabbit (jointed) on both sides. Add boiling water, cucumber and salt, and simmer for about half an hour. Mix the flour carefully in a little milk, strain into the casserole, and continue simmering for about an hour or until the rabbit is tender. The length of cooking depends on the age of the rabbit. Be careful that the sauce does not stick once the flour is in. You must stir from time to time. If you can spare and afford about half a teacup of cream you can add it to the casserole a few minutes before serving; at the same time add the pepper.

This is a nice white dish of rabbit to which spiced cucumbers add a subtle piquancy. Rabbit has approximately the same nutritional value as meat, but needs the addition of fat in some form to bring up the calorie value as the flesh is rather dry. Cucumbers are not very easy to digest and some people can't cope with them at all, so bear this in mind when planning a meal to include this recipe. As accompaniments, I would suggest creamed potato with chopped chives added, and either green peas and carrots or brussels sprouts.

Rabbit Cream

1 oz. butter
1½ ozs. self-raising flour
½ pint milk
Salt, pepper
About 2 cupsful minced and pounded cooked rabbit
1 egg
A little grated nutmeg

Melt butter, stir in flour and add milk gradually, stirring all the time until the mixture thickens. Remove from the heat and add the rabbit, egg, seasoning and nutmeg. Mix well. Steam for about 1½ hours in a greased pudding basin. Turn out and serve with any nice sauce. Tomato sauce (see page 141) will do very well when in season. You can steam in a soufflé dish and serve without turning out if you prefer.

This basic recipe can be used for any minced and pounded meat or fish, though for fish I would omit the nutmeg and add a little chopped parsley. The egg coagulates on exposure to moist heat and binds the mixture. This cream can be given to an invalid, as it slips down easily and can be made to look very attractive if turned out and garnished prettily with the sauce poured around. Tomato sauce might be a little rich for a delicate digestion, so I would play safe and serve a nice glossy cream sauce and get your colour from the accompanying vegetables.

Raised Pie

½ lb. flour
2 ozs. lard
¼ pint water
1 egg
Salt, pepper to taste

½ lb. meat
4 ozs. bacon or ham
1 onion
1 dessertspoon mixed herbs

Boil the water and lard, mix with the flour. Knead well, roll out and line a 1 lb. cake tin (an oblong one is best) keeping a bit back for the lid. The filling can be made with rabbit, chicken, veal, pigeon, or any game previously cooked and minced with the bacon – in the case of veal it is better to use ham. Mince the onion, add it and the herbs to the meat. Season to taste. Hard-boil the egg (see page 19) and shell it. Put a thin layer of the mince in the bottom of the cake tin, add the egg and fill up all round and over the top with the mince. Put on a lid of pastry, pinch the edges together with the rest of the pastry. Decorate with a few odd pieces, making leaves or flowers, brush over with a little egg or milk and bake in a moderate oven for about an hour. Turn out of the tin when cold. This pie is very easy to make and looks extremely professional.

◆ ❖ ◆

I have often wondered why we don't use a raised pie crust more, it is very economical on fat, and is just as good cold – perhaps even better – as hot, which is not the case with most pastry. The rules for hot water crust are the reverse for other pastries, as everything should be warm instead of cold. The success depends on kneading quickly before the water cools. You'll have to use a wooden spoon to start with or you'll burn your hands. The dough must be fairly stiff but not so stiff as to be brittle. Special pie tins are available which have a hinge at the sides to facilitate unmoulding. If you cannot get one of these, use a cake tin with a loose bottom or mould over a bottle or jar and bake with a piece of double paper pinned around. A little jelly stock added after baking improves the pie.

Vol-au-Vent

4 ozs. self-raising flour
3 ozs. fat
For the filling see below

Make some rough puff pastry according to the recipe on page 15. Roll out about half inch thick, cut into two large rounds with a large cutter or the edge of a flan ring or cake tin. Make a cut about quarter inch deep with a smaller cutter about an inch inside the other one. Bake in a hot oven. Remove and lift out the inside round with a knife. Scoop out a little of the pastry and fill. Put the lid on top of the filling and return to the oven for a few minutes.

You can fill with any scraps you have handy, e.g. chopped chicken and ham with perhaps a few peas in a béchamel sauce (see page 129); chopped veal and mushrooms in a brown sauce; finnan haddock and scrambled egg. Have the filling hot and not too runny. You can, if you like, make small vol-au-vents, one for each person, but one for two or three is much less trouble and just as good. You can also make the cases a day or two beforehand. Keep them in a tin and heat up when required.

Nothing is more delicious than these crisp pastry puffs with a nice creamy filling, which can be sweet as well as savoury. The tricky part is the baking. You need a very hot oven to bring the pastry up quickly and set the gluten in the flour. But as the pastry is fairly thick, and has to cook right through, place on a baking sheet brushed over with water, this will prevent burning. Keep the rounds in the middle of the tin in the centre of the highest oven shelf, if the tops are browning too quickly, put a piece of paper sprinkled with water over them. Avoid opening the door until the vol-au-vents are well set. Depending on size, they should take from 30-40 minutes to cook. Piercing the centre of the rounds with a fine skewer before baking helps them to rise evenly.

VEGETABLES
AND SALAD

Aubergine a l'Americaine

2 aubergines
4 tablespoons butter
1 onion finely chopped
1½ tablespoons finely chopped parsley
Some brown breadcrumbs

Cut the aubergines into cubes and cook in a small amount of boiling water until soft. Drain. Cook the onion in butter until golden brown, then add the aubergine and parsley. Put the mixture into a buttered baking dish. Melt the rest of the butter and add the breadcrumbs. Spread on top of the aubergine mixture. Bake in a moderately hot oven until nicely browned. This can be made beforehand and heated up (about half an hour) before serving.

◆ ❖ ◆

Aubergines or egg plants belong to the vegetable marrow family, they are very delicately flavoured and need careful cooking. They vary in colour from white to yellow, and from dark purple to red. The purple ones are considered the best. The seeds must be removed before cooking. Aubergines are eaten a lot in France but are rather expensive over here. Food value, not very high, but lack of calories can be made up if you incorporate fat and other ingredients in the cooking.

Cauliflower
with Dutch Sauce

1 cauliflower
Dutch sauce

Steam the cauliflower in about an inch of water. Be careful that all the water does not boil away. See that the cauliflower is not over-boiled by prodding with a fork from time to time. A medium one takes about 20 minutes. Serve cold with Dutch sauce (see page 132).

There are two schools of thought on cooking cauliflower. One says that it should be cooked slowly so as to prevent the flower from breaking, the stalk being pierced with a skewer to ensure thorough cooking. The new school of thought tells you to divide the cauliflower into flowerettes and boil briskly in the minimum of water, so preserving as much of the soluble mineral content as possible. Personally I like to see a nice firm cauliflower draped with a good sauce, so I follow the first method, compromising by removing the green stalks and cooking separately as for cabbage.

Cucumber Salad

Peel the cucumber, cut with a cutter or by hand into very thin slices. Put the slices singly and flat on a large plate or dish, not over-lapping. Sprinkle with salt. Stand the plate on its side against a wall on the draining board (or put something under it to·catch the moisture). Leave for an hour or so and you will find that a lot of water has drained out. Cover with a French dressing with no salt in it and serve.

Cucumbers are indigestible because they are hard and need a lot of work by the gastric juices that break them down. Some people think that leaving the skin on improves their digestibility. The custom of draining off the water from the cucumber, as directed in this recipe, is not essential, and in my opinion it seems rather like draining the juice from any ripe fruit. A quick way to trim cucumbers is to draw the prongs of a fork sharply down the sides all round, this gives an attractive crimped appearance to the edges when sliced.

Hungarian Vegetable Marrow

1 marrow (about 2 lbs.)
2 ozs. lard
4 tablespoons flour
4 tablespoons sour cream
1 tablespoon dill seeds or some sprigs of fresh dill
2 tablespoons paprika, a little salt

Peel the marrow, take out the seeds and cut into pieces as for straw potatoes (the Hungarians have a cutter for this rather like a cucumber slicer but I have not seen one in England). Sprinkle with salt and leave for at least half an hour. Melt the lard on a low heat, add the flour, stir well. Squeeze the water out of the marrow before adding it to the mixture. If you can get any fresh dill (sometimes it can be procured in Soho) throw in a few sprigs, otherwise pour a little boiling water on the dill seeds, leave to soak for an hour or two, and then strain the water on to the marrow, etc. Add the paprika and salt and a tumbler of boiling water gradually. Simmer the mixture until the marrow is soft, about 30 minutes, stirring from time to time so that it does not stick. Add the sour cream just before serving and remove the dill if you have used it.

◆ ❖ ◆

Marrow contains 94.8% water so you will see that it has little food value. However, marrows are refreshing, and if cooked carefully and not allowed to go mushy, provide variety to the menu. This recipe is good because it has plenty of flavour and the result is a nice creamy mixture which goes very well with a dry main course, such as grilled or baked cutlets or fish. I had not used dill seeds in cooking until I tried out this recipe but it gave an unusual peppermint tang to the marrow, which I liked very much.

Petits Pois à la Française

3 lbs. peas
A small lettuce
5 or 6 button onions or 1 medium one chopped
1 or 2 lumps of sugar
2 ozs. butter
Salt, pepper

Shell the peas, put them in a saucepan with all the other ingredients (the lettuce should be cut into strips). Just cover with water, cook with the lid on until the peas are cooked and most of the water has evaporated so that the juice is thick enough for the whole to cohere. This is a very good way of cooking not very good peas, as it makes them taste sweet and tender, but it always seems to me a pity to spoil the best English garden peas (which are so delicious boiled plain) by adding all the other ingredients. Tinned peas can also be cooked à la Française, only in that case cook them in the water in which they have been preserved, and not very much of that.

◆ ❖ ◆

Peas contain second-class protein and are a valuable addition to the diet. Green peas also contain Vitamin C, sugar and mineral salts. There are many delicious ways of cooking them and the recipe given is a classic. I agree, however, that it is hard to beat young peas plain cooked with mint and sugar. Peas sometimes have a habit of being obstinately tough. The skin of the pea is the snag and overcooking doesn't help. The surest way to avoid this is to blanch them for a minute or two, strain and put in the oven in a covered casserole with 1 oz. of butter to 2 lbs. of peas, 1 teaspoon of sugar, a pinch of salt and very little water; they take a little longer to cook but will be as tender as you could wish.

Red Cabbage

1 medium-sized red cabbage
4 tablespoons vinegar
2 tablespoons brown sugar
2 teaspoons powdered cinnamon
Salt, pepper

Cut the cabbage into shreds, wash and put into a saucepan with 1½ teacups water and all the other ingredients. Cook slowly for about an hour, stirring occasionally. This tastes rather exotic and everyone may not like it, so it should only be given to guests who like strange foods!

This vegetable is usually pickled in this country, although it can be cooked by any method used for ordinary cabbage, but as it is a much closer plant and contains more cellulose (fibrous framework, or roughage) than the green variety, it takes much longer to cook. Dietically, it contains minerals and Vitamin C but not to such a degree as green-leaved vegetables. If you do not fancy the cinnamon, omit it and add a large sour apple and a few raisins. Red cabbage is good with grilled sausages.

Snow Soufflé

2 eggs
6 ozs. mashed potatoes
6 ozs. cooked cauliflower (flower only)
2 ozs. butter
2 teaspoons chopped parsley
Salt, pepper

Separate the yolk and white of the eggs. Beat yolks well and stir in potatoes, butter and parsley. Mix well and add the cauliflower (well mashed or minced) and the seasoning. Beat the whites very stiff and fold in carefully. Pour into a greased soufflé dish and bake in a moderate oven for half an hour. As there is less egg in this soufflé than in most it will not rise quite so much, so fill up your dish or it will look as if it had not risen at all!

◆ ❖ ◆

Soufflé is a delicious sounding word – the very sound conjuring up something light and fluffy, as a soufflé should be. They are not difficult to make, being merely some sort of creamy mixture (usually thick white sauce), either sweet or savoury, made to rise by the addition of eggs, the stiffly whisked whites incorporating air into the mixture, and giving it a characteristic spongy consistency. Dried eggs can be used if you sift in a heaped teaspoon of baking powder to each egg at the last moment. This is quite a filling dish, the quantities given for four portions providing about 260 calories each.

Stuffed Aubergine

Take two medium-sized aubergines (the purple sort is tastier than the white egg plant). Cut in half lengthwise and take out the seeds. Score with a knife several times but be careful not to damage the outer skin. Place in a greased baking tin, cover with greased paper and bake in a moderate oven for about a quarter of an hour. Take out and scoop out the insides, leaving just the shells. Put the flesh into a basin and to each breakfast cupful of aubergine add a teaspoon of chopped onion, a tablespoon of chopped ham, two tablespoons breadcrumbs and one chopped mushroom. Season and mix with gravy or tomato purée and put the mixture back into the empty skins. Sprinkle with brown breadcrumbs, put a few small dabs of butter on the top and bake for 15-20 minutes. All this can be prepared beforehand and just heated up in time to serve.

◆ ❖ ◆

I suggest serving these as an 'Entremet' to follow the main course. They not only look attractive in their pretty purple skin, but are unusual and would turn an otherwise ordinary meal into something special. Simple to prepare, they would give you extra time for the main course, or for that necessary 'tidy up' before the guests arrive. They would also be very good with a steamed chicken and egg sauce.

Braised Lettuce

Put a cos lettuce in a casserole with a small lump of fat, a lump of sugar and about half a teacup of stock, or water in which you have melted a mustard spoon of Marmite and a little salt. Cook slowly on the top of the stove or in the oven for 1 to 1½ hours (it must, of course, depend on the size of the lettuce) until the lettuce is quite soft all through.

I don't recommend cooking lettuces as you lose all the Vitamin C and minerals. However, having made that point, there is no reason why you shouldn't serve them this way if you make up the vitamin deficiency with something else. Actually there is far more Vitamin C in watercress and parsley than in lettuce. I said before that it is the dark green leaves that contain the goodness and the nicest lettuces are usually on the pale side.

Marrow Stew

1 medium sized marrow
2 onions
4 tomatoes
A piece of butter the size of an egg
Salt, pepper

Peel the marrow, remove the seeds and slice, put in a casserole with the peeled tomatoes, the butter and the sliced onions. Add a little water and cook slowly for 1½ hours. Just before serving add salt and pepper.

It doesn't need much ingenuity to adapt this dish into something quite substantial. Diced bacon or ham, smoked haddock or rice previously fried in butter with a little stock added, would be good variants; alternatively grated cheese and breadcrumbs added at the end of the baking and browned under the grill would be nice.

SWEETS

Apple and Quince Mould

1 lb. apples
1 lb. quinces
2 tablespoons sugar
½ oz. gelatine

Peel and core the fruit. Cut into small slices, add a little water and the sugar and cook until the water is absorbed and the fruit soft. Stir frequently to prevent it catching. Beat well with a fork or whisk until there are no lumps left. Melt the gelatine in a little water and add to the fruit. Mix well and pour into a basin. Leave overnight or put into the refrigerator to harden. Stand the basin in hot water for a second before turning out.

You will find that quinces take much longer to cook than apples, so allow half an hour at least to soften them, and then add the apple with a little more water if necessary. Another 5-10 minutes should make the fruit soft and mushy. If you put your sugar in at the last moment it will be less likely to burn. Colour is important with cold sweets. A drop or two of apple-green colour or cochineal will improve the appearance, and if you want your mould to set quickly pour into individual dishes. Cool in a basin of ice cubes and put into the refrigerator to harden. Use angelica or chopped crystallised ginger and whipped cream to decorate.

Apple Flan

Short pastry made with 1 oz. fat and 1½ ozs. flour
1 lb. cooking apples
2 tablespoons apricot jam

Line a flan ring or sandwich tin with pastry; make a few holes in the bottom with a skewer or fork, bake for quarter of an hour until hard but not coloured. Take out of the oven. Put one apple to one side then peel and core the rest and cut into small pieces. Put these into a saucepan with very little water. Cook, stirring frequently until all the water is absorbed and the apples are a stiff purée. Peel and core the single apple and slice very thinly. Cut each slice in half. Fill the flan with the purée. Lay the slices neatly on the top, in a circle, slightly overlapping. Melt the jam and pour on to the flan through a strainer so that no solid lumps are used. Spread with a palette knife and return to a hot oven for 10-15 minutes when the apple slices will be cooked and the pastry a golden brown. Serve hot or cold. This makes a very elegant looking party sweet and is really very easy to make. One of those flan rings with an edge that comes off with the removal of a pin is a great help, as it is extremely difficult to remove flans from their tins without spoiling them.

◆ ❖ ◆

The quantities given for pastry in these recipes seem very small, and are, in fact, just sufficient for four portions if you roll your dough very thin, which needs a fair amount of care or it will break. To be on the safe side, I suggest you increase your amounts by half; any left-over pastry can be made into pastry cases, which are awfully useful for last minute sweets. It is far more economical to stew apples the French way, that is to simply wash them and remove any bruised parts and pop them whole (or cut into three if you are in a hurry) into a pan with a little water, cover and simmer until soft – about 45 minutes. Break up with a wooden or silver spoon and sieve. You will have a lovely thick purée with a good rich flavour, and all that will be left in the sieve will be the apple cores and stalks.

Apple Slices

2 ozs. self-raising flour
1½ ozs. fat
A drop of egg or milk
½ lb. small cooking apples
2 or 3 tablespoons apricot jam

Make a rough puff paste (see page 15) and roll out very thin. Cut out a narrow oblong about a foot long. Fold over each end about one inch. Paint the ends and about an inch along each side with egg or milk. Cut an inch wide strip of pastry for each side and stick on. Paint on top of these and repeat. Put a strip of pastry on to each folded-over end. Paint all the edge pieces. Make a few holes in the bottom with a skewer to prevent it rising and bake in a hot oven until just cooked but not brown. In the meantime peel and core one apple and cut into paper thin slices. Make the rest of the apple into a purée with very little water. Remove the pastry from the oven. Put a thin layer of purée in the middle and cover with the apple rings cut in half and overlapping. They should be laid across the width not the length of the pastry. Heat the jam and spread a thin layer carefully over the apple slices. Return to the oven and cook a few minutes until the apple is done. Remove from the oven and cut into slices 1½ to 2 inches wide when cold. This is a good tea-party or dinner sweet.

Any fruit purée could be used for this dish – rhubarb flavoured with ground ginger and sultanas, with a few even-sized pieces left for decoration, and cherry or plum jam instead of apricot. Strawberries stiffened with a little arrowroot would be lovely, or blackcurrant purée with plenty of whipped cream. So far as vitamin value goes, blackcurrants come way at the top of the list – 1 oz. containing more than one days requirements; the citrus family come next, and then strawberries and gooseberries. Cooking destroys this vitamin, so it is better, whenever possible, to serve fruit fresh. To get the maximum nutriment, eat green stuff and fruit within a short time of picking, as the vitamin content gradually deteriorates.

Bakewell Pudding

4-5 ozs. puff pastry or short
1½ ozs. ground almonds
1½ ozs. sugar
2 ozs. butter
A little grated lemon peel
2 baked sieved potatoes
2 eggs (leave out the white of one)
A few spoonsful of raspberry jam

Line a pie dish or flan ring with puff or short pastry. Mix the almonds, sugar, butter, eggs and potatoes well together. Put a layer of the jam in the bottom of the dish, then a little grated lemon peel and lastly the almond mixture. Bake in a moderate oven for 40 minutes. Serve warm but not hot.

◆ ❖ ◆

I prefer lemon curd to line the pastry case of a bakewell pudding, but any jam will do. If you haven't any ground almonds use 4 ozs. of soya flour, omit the potato and add 1 teaspoon of almond essence. Soya flour is very nourishing as it contains protein and fat, so use it whenever possible, especially in children's food. Keep some pastry trimmings back to decorate the top and add blanched almonds just before taking out of the oven. Your potato, after sieving, should weigh about 3 ozs.

Caramel Cream

½ pint milk
2 eggs
A little caster sugar
A handful of burnt almonds
2 ozs. loaf sugar
¼ oz. gelatine
½ pint cream

Make a custard with the milk, the two egg yolks and the caster sugar to taste. Make a caramel by boiling the loaf sugar with three tablespoons of water until it goes brown, then add a little more water and boil up. Mix the caramel and the custard. Dissolve the gelatine in a little hot water and strain into the mixture. Next add the whipped cream and the whipped egg whites carefully. Whisk the whole mixture together until nearly set. Be very careful about this. If you whisk too long the cream will be full of lumps of gelatine. If you stop too soon all the liquid goes to the bottom and the froth remains on the top; the latter is, of course, the lesser evil. Pour into a soufflé dish and cover with burnt almonds.

This is one of the best recipes in the book and though it takes a little time to prepare it is well worth it. The cream, whipped egg whites and gelatine give the pudding a lovely frothy consistency which melts in the mouth. To burn almonds, blanch and bake in the oven until a nice brown, shaking the tin occasionally. For a more economical caramel cream, you can coat a plain dry mould with caramel, using only 1 tablespoon of water, and fill up with a cream made by thickening 1 pt. of milk (sweetened and flavoured with lemon rind) with 2 ozs. of ground rice. Turn out when cold.

Caramel Pudding

1 level tablespoon sugar
3 eggs
½ pint milk
A few drops of vanilla essence

Grease a pudding or cake tin. Melt the sugar in it and let it run over the bottom and sides of the tin then harden. Mix the eggs and milk thoroughly, add the vanilla and pour into the caramelled tin. Cover and put into a basin of cold water, bring to the boil and steam slowly for an hour. Like all custards, this pudding must not be allowed to boil or it will curdle. Turn out while still hot but serve cold.

Here you have a very nourishing and easily digested pudding which provides 560 calories. If you wish you could steam it in individual dariole tins. The safest way to prevent a custard from cooking too fast is to have the steamer half off the flame, with the custard on the side away from the heat; the water will just simmer which is all the heat that is needed to coagulate the protein in the egg and set the custard.

Castle Puddings
with Sabayon Sauce

4 ozs. butter
4 ozs. granulated or caster sugar
2 eggs
4 ozs. self-raising flour

Mix the sugar and butter, beat to a cream (the quickest way to do this in cold weather is with your hand, as the heat of the hand melts the butter). Add the eggs, mix well. Sift in the flour and mix again. Cook in greased castle pudding moulds in a fairly hot oven for 20-30 minutes. Turn out and serve with sabayon sauce (see page 139). You can make the castle puddings beforehand and heat up just before serving.

◆ ❖ ◆

The rich sponge mixture given in this recipe is a basic sponge which can be baked as a cake with flavouring like lemon, orange or almond, or with dried fruit and spice, or whatever else you fancy. The mixture can be steamed in a greased basin (this sized pudding would need 1-1½ hours.). Any sauce can be used, warmed syrup or jam are good. If you wish, you can put a little jam at the bottom of the basin. This is almost as good if you halve the quantities of fat, sugar and egg, and add 3 tablespoons of milk. Fold in the flour as lightly and quickly as possible. The golden rule for creamed mixtures is to beat really hard until all the liquid is added, and then be as light as a fairy in adding the flour.

Cherry Flan

Short pastry made with ¾ oz. lard
1½ ozs. self-raising flour
Sugar to taste
1½ tablespoons cornflour
¾ lb. morello cherries

Line a flan tin with the pastry. Prick all over the bottom. Fill with rice or split peas to keep from rising and cook for about 12 minutes in a medium oven. (The rice or peas can be used over and over again.) In the meantime stone the cherries (the easiest way is with a hair-pin), stew them for about 5 minutes in very little water and sugar to taste. Strain off the juice and add 8 tablespoons of it to the cornflour which you have previously mixed with a little cold water. Boil for about 3 minutes, stirring all the time. Arrange the cherries in the flan tin and pour the cornflour through a strainer on the top of them. The most convenient flan tins undo at the side and take to pieces; if you cannot get one of these you have to use a round sandwich tin, and great care must be taken when taking the flan out of it or you will break it. Take the flan out before you fill it. A touch of Kirsch in the fruit juice is an improvement.

◆ ❖ ◆

I prefer using arrowroot for thickening a fruit syrup. It is more expensive than cornflour, but in my opinion, makes a clearer, glossier syrup. It helps if you line your baking tin with paper if you haven't a flan ring; you'll find it much easier to take out, and always line the flan itself with greased paper (butterside down) before filling with split peas, or you'll find they will sink into the pastry and be tedious to remove. Cherries contain some calcium and iron, though not very much Vitamin C.

Fraises Paillard

2 lbs. strawberries
½ pint cream
Sugar to taste

Pick out about two dozen of the best strawberries; of these keep a few
to decorate the top of the sweet. Cut the rest in half. Put the remaining
strawberries through a sieve. Whip the cream very stiff and mix with the
purée of strawberries and sugar to taste. Add the cut-up fruit. Pour into
a soufflé dish, decorate with the whole strawberries and serve well iced.

*The way to whip cream is to put the required amount of double cream
in a basin in a bowl of ice and with an egg whisk beat really hard until it
begins to thicken; then slow down as at this stage it stiffens rapidly and
may lose the smooth texture. Add sugar and flavouring carefully at the end
of the whipping or it may curdle. Double cream is best but single cream
will do if you add one egg white to each pint of cream. There is calcium,
iron and Vitamin C in strawberries, and as thick cream is almost all fat of
the most easily digested kind (providing 1,800 calories per ½ pint) you can
see how good this sweet is for you.*

Milanese Soufflé
(Orange or Lemon)

3 eggs
3 ozs. caster sugar
Juice of 2 lemons or oranges
Rind of 1 lemon or orange
½ pint cream
Vanilla to taste
½ oz. gelatine
¼ pint white wine or water

Whisk yolks, sugar and juice in a double saucepan over boiling water until light and thick. Add the grated rind and allow to cool. Whisk the cream and add a few drops of vanilla. Dissolve the gelatine in the water. Whisk the whites very stiff; strain the gelatine, etc. into the yolks, then the cream, and lastly fold in the whites. The mixture should set almost immediately. This is enough for eight people, but is a little difficult to divide because of the three eggs.

Although this sweet is called a soufflé it is actually not one in the ordinary sense of the word as it is not cooked after the whites are added. It is really a mousse enriched with yolks of eggs, called a soufflé because of the characteristic spongy consistency. Your success in making this depends on the care you have taken in whisking the egg whites, which should be very stiff. Do your whisking with everything as cold as possible, a pinch of salt helps, and you won't get a really stiff froth unless you use really fresh eggs. Orange is inclined to be insipid in flavour so add a drop or two of lemon juice which will give it a little sharpness.

Miller's Pudding

4 ozs. sugar
4 ozs. butter
4 ozs. flour
½ teaspoon bicarbonate of soda
2 eggs
2 tablespoons strawberry jam

Mix the butter and sugar well together, then mix the soda with the flour. Add the eggs to the butter and sugar and gradually add the flour; lastly mix in the jam. Put the mixture in a greased pudding basin and steam for 1½ hours. Do not fill the basin more than about half full as this pudding rises a good deal. Serve with whipped cream. You can cook and serve in a soufflé dish and not risk the turning out and collapsing at the last minute, which is always such agony for the cook-hostess.

This is the same basic mixture as the castle pudding recipe, but the raising agent is different, as you use bi-carb instead of baking powder which makes the pudding a rich brown colour. If you run a knife round the sides of the basin and leave for 3 minutes before turning out, you will find that your pudding will turn out all in one piece. It looks so nice on the dish with a blob of whipped cream on top, though I prefer a hot sauce with steamed puddings. For this one I'd choose hot strawberry jam with a dash of sherry or lemon juice. For plainer days, custard would do.

Pancakes

6 tablespoons flour
6 tablespoons milk
4 eggs

Put the flour in a basin, break in the eggs and mix one by one. Beat well so that there are no lumps. Add the milk gradually. Pancake mixture should be of the consistency of thin cream and is all the better if it is left standing a few hours before use. Brush a frying pan with melted butter, heat until very hot. Dip a small cup into the pancake mixture and pour sufficient of it into the frying pan to cover it very thinly. When lightly brown on one side turn over with a palette knife and cook the other side (or toss if you prefer!) Roll up and keep hot until all the mixture is cooked. Serve with brown sugar and lemon, or jam. It is important to make the pancakes very thin.

◆ ❖ ◆

This is a much richer batter than I generally use, mine being 1 egg and ½ pint of milk to 4 ozs. of flour, but of course pancakes made from this much eggier mixture are far richer and more nutritious. You will find that a small cup or wine glass of batter is ample for each pancake. Never keep pancakes warm in the oven or they'll be hard and leathery; they should be eaten straight out of the pan for perfection, but if they must wait I have found that the best way to keep them hot is to put flat on top of each other between two warm plates. For your information: crêpes are especially thin pancakes filled with a savoury mixture such as creamed chicken or lobster, or served with lighted brandy or other spirit as a sweet dish.

Pêches au Mareschino

A dozen peaches
A little caster sugar to taste
About 6 tablespoons maraschino or Kirsch (more if you can afford it)

This is an excellent sweet when the South African peaches are in season. Dip each peach into boiling water; skin, stone and cut into quarters. Put in a glass dish, dust lightly with sugar to bring out the flavour and sprinkle with the liqueur. Leave for a few hours before serving, turning over at least once, so that the fruit is thoroughly impregnated with the liqueur.

Peaches contain a lot of Vitamin A so console yourself with this when you are being extravagant over them and feel you shouldn't. As they are such a luxury fruit one seldom feels inclined to use them other than whole, but if you have the means or the opportunity to use them liberally, they are quite delicious made into a fool as directed on page 126.

Queen of Puddings

1 pint milk
3 tablespoons semolina
Cocoa to taste
2 eggs
8 tablespoons caster sugar
Jam

Boil the milk. Sprinkle in the semolina slowly so that it does not go lumpy. Stir well, bring to the boil again and cook for about 3 minutes. Take off the heat. Add four tablespoons sugar and cocoa to taste. Now stir in the yolks of the eggs. Put in a pie dish, allow to cool and spread with jam; this takes quite a lot of jam but if you can spare it it is much nicer thickly spread. Whisk the whites of the eggs until quite stiff and stir in the remainder of the sugar very carefully. Spread over the jam and cook in a cool oven until hard. This sweet is delicious hot or cold.

◆ ❖ ◆

Another method is to use 5 ozs. of white breadcrumbs instead of the semolina, and flavour with lemon or vanilla. This is actually what most people understand as Queen of Puddings, and it is a good way of using up bread, but the chocolate variety is, I think, nicer. Very popular with children, it looks expensive but actually costs very little. I particularly recommend apricot jam, which you should cook in the oven, Regulo 5, 350° F. for half an hour before adding the meringue, when you should reduce the heat.

Steamed Semolina Pudding

1 pint milk
4 tablespoons semolina
2 eggs
A handful of sultanas

Bring the milk to the boil and gradually throw in the semolina, stirring all the time so that it does not form into lumps. Cook for 2 or 3 minutes after the semolina is all in, by which time it will thicken. Now mix in the beaten-up eggs (off the heat) and the sultanas. Put into a well-greased pudding basin, cover with greased paper or a lid, and steam for 1½ hours. Turn out and serve with sabayon sauce (see page 139).

Semolina is made from wheat and is technically termed a small grain cereal, there being three classes: whole-rice, barley and tapioca; medium-semolina and sago; and powdered grain cornflour, round rice and arrowroot. The first class should be soaked for a short time in milk before cooking to soften the tough outer skin. The second class needs boiling for 15-20 minutes until the grain is soft and transparent, and with fine grain cereals the milk should be heated and poured onto the grain, previously mixed to a cream with a little cold milk; it should then be boiled for 10 minutes. These are minimum times required to make the grain digestible; it can, of course, be baked or steamed for a longer period according to taste.

Swiss Apple Tart

2 lbs. apples
Sugar to taste
½ teaspoon cinnamon
1 teaspoon mixed spice
1 handful sultanas
2 ozs. lard or butter
4 ozs. self-raising flour

Peel, core and chop the apples. Cook in very little water. When partly cooked add the sugar, sultanas and spice. Continue cooking, stirring frequently, until the water is absorbed and the fruit has become a purée. Leave to cool. Make some short pastry (see page 13). Roll out thin. Line an oblong cake tin or small sandwich tin with the pastry. Fill with the apple mixture, not quite to the top of the tin. Cover with a layer of pastry and fold over the two edges pinched together. Bake in a fairly hot oven. Turn out when cold. Or cut into squares before removing from the tin. In any case this tart is nicer cold and must be made with a very stiff apple purée or is inclined to become soggy.

◆ ❖ ◆

I think it improves this tart if you sprinkle sugar and cinnamon on top of the pastry about 10 minutes before it is cooked, this gives a nice toffee-like appearance. The north country idea of serving fruit tarts for tea is an excellent one, slabs of this tart soon disappear when the children come home hungry, and it makes a change from cake. The hot oven necessary for this sweet is likely to force the apple out of the edges unless you seal them very firmly. Always prick the top of a filled pastry dish so that the steam may escape – flour your fork and you'll get a clean incision.

Chocolate Marie

1½ ozs. chocolate per head
1 egg per head

Melt chocolate in a double saucepan. Add the yolks of the eggs, mix well. When cool add the whisked whites carefully. Serve in glasses with a dollop of whipped cream on the top of each. Or you can sprinkle with chopped and roasted almonds or hazelnuts, or decorate with crystallised violet or rose leaves and pieces of walnut.

When you are melting chocolate for a sweet of this kind, break it up roughly first and melt it fairly slowly or it may burn. If you haven't a double saucepan, a basin in a pan of hot water will do as well. Chocolate is very nourishing as it contains a high proportion of fat. One portion of chocolate marie provides as many calories as half a pound of fried fish, so beware all you would-be slims! You should hand some sort of crisp biscuit with a rich sweet of this kind.

Figues Flambées

Peel some fresh figs and put them in a metal pan over a medium flame with a mixture of two parts curaçao and one part brandy, and just a little sugar. Set the liqueurs alight and prick the figs with a fork while the liqueurs burn, shaking the pan meanwhile. By the time the figs are warm and soft the flame dies out naturally. Serve at once.

This should really be cooked on the dining room table in a chafing dish, as part of the enjoyment of this sweet is to see the pretty blue flame.
A rather expensive pudding unless you have a fig tree in the garden, as you will need three figs per portion, and sufficient spirit to soak well into the fruit, about ½ gill for six figs. Figs contain a lot of calcium.

Fool

This can be made with any soft fruit or plums. The fruit should be sieved, then add an equal quantity of whipped cream (or two parts fruit to one part custard and one part whipped cream) and sugar to taste. Serve in custard glasses, preferably well iced.

◆ ❖ ◆

When preparing fruit for cooking, much the best way of removing stalks is with a pair of scissors. Rhubarb and ginger makes a lovely fool, though some people prefer a touch of vanilla. Try mixing fruits: raspberries with redcurrants, apples with rhubarb or damsons. A little gelatine will help to stiffen the cream if you haven't time to whip it. A hair sieve should be used for fruit, metal sieves are inclined to make the fruit taste. Serve with sponge fingers.

Spiced Apples

3 lbs. apples
Sugar to taste
¾ teaspoon cinnamon
1½ teaspoons mixed spice
1½ handfuls sultanas or currants or both

Peel, core and chop the apples. Cook in a little water. When partly cooked add the sugar, spice and sultanas. Finish cooking, stirring frequently until the apples have become a purée. Serve in individual glasses.

Here again I suggest stewing your apples whole, as explained in my notes on apple flan (see page 109). Apple purée can be bottled when apples are plentiful so as to be on hand whenever needed. I bottled a very thick unsweetened purée regularly through the war, adding sugar, water and flavouring as I wanted it, for pies, fools, and apple sauce. We had it for breakfast too, and I've served it as a drink diluted with rhubarb or plum syrup.

SAUCES

Béchamel or White Sauce

A piece of butter the size of an egg
1 heaped tablespoon flour
½ pint milk
Salt, pepper

Melt the butter over a moderate heat; add the flour and stir until well mixed. Now add the milk very slowly or the sauce will get lumpy and you will have to strain it. Go on stirring until all the milk has been added and the sauce is the consistency of thick cream. To reheat béchamel it is advisable to add a further drop of milk.

If you have any pretension to being a cook at all you must be able to make a smooth glossy sauce. It is easy if you remember three things –
(1) allow your flour to cook in the fat for a minute or two until the bottom of the pan has a honeycomb look, this bursts the starch grains in the flour and makes it absorbent; (2) draw your pan off the heat and allow to cool slightly before adding the liquid, which shouldn't fizzle up and go into lumps at this stage, but mix smoothly with the roux; (3) stir all the time, one simply cannot leave a thick sauce until it is cooked. To get a nice gloss, remove from heat and beat with a wooden spoon.

Chocolate Sauce

Add a knob of butter to 4 ozs. of chocolate and a tumbler of water and simmer until thick. This sauce can be reheated.

◆ ❖ ◆

Melt the chocolate in a double saucepan and then add the butter and water – hot water will save time. This is much the best way of making chocolate sauce if you have the chocolate, but for plainer fare an ordinary custard powder made with boiled cocoa is quite adequate and simple to make.

Cheese Sauce

2 egg yolks
½ pint milk
2 'Swiss Gruyères'
Piece of butter the size of an egg
Salt, pepper

Mix the yolks and the milk, add the cheese cut into small pieces and the other ingredients. Cook on a low heat, stirring all the time until thick and creamy. Serve immediately.

◆ ❖ ◆

I have said several times how nutritious a food cheese is, containing more protein than any other, so it is hardly necessary for me to add that a cheese sauce (particularly this one which has the added protein of the egg yolks) can turn any vegetable or cereal dish with which it is used, into a main course. The high proportion of fat in cheese, which when heated forms a fatty acid round the casein (cheese protein) makes it difficult for the digestive juices to break down, but if you add a good pinch of bi-carbonate of potash to every 4 ozs. of cheese, it counteracts the irritating fatty acids and makes it more digestible.

Dutch Sauce

Whisk two eggs with a little vinegar (tarragon is the best for this sauce if you like the flavour). Add a teaspoonful or so of sugar to taste, salt and pepper. Cook on a low heat, whisking continually until it thickens. Do not let it boil or, like custard, it will curdle. Remove from the heat and add gradually a piece of butter the size of a walnut and a little cream or milk. Can be used hot or cold and is an excellent substitute for mayonnaise.

I think this is better if you use yolks of the eggs only, and I prefer to boil two tablespoons of vinegar and lemon juice together until reduced by half, cool, and add the eggs separately. However, we all prefer the familiar, and no doubt you may think the method given here simpler. This sauce is also called Hollandaise: serve it with meat, fish or vegetables, in fact anything that needs a sharp sauce.

Custard

1 egg
½ pint milk
Sugar to taste
Vanilla essence

Whisk the egg until the white and the yolk are well mixed. Add the milk, sugar and a few drops of vanilla. I have always found that Marshall's is the best essence to use. Whisk all together. Now put over a low heat and whisk hard until it begins to thicken. Stir with a wooden spoon until it is quite thick. Be very careful that it does not catch on the bottom of the saucepan and do not let it boil or it will curdle.

In other words, the invalid's egg and milk heated – nothing simpler or better for you. A custard should always be given to children with their puddings, as it adds calcium, iron and Vitamins A and B. When cool it thickens – never take off the skin, it is the fat which has risen to the top of the liquid. A cold custard is improved if you beat in a little cream.

Brandy Butter

Mix 2 ozs. of butter with 3 ozs. of icing sugar. As it is always at Christmas that one makes this sauce and the butter is therefore very hard, it is advisable to leave it in a warm place first, but do not let it melt. The easiest way to mix is with the hand. When thoroughly mixed add brandy to taste. Can be left to set fairly hard again and cut into squares; or served looking like whipped cream

This is sometimes called 'Hard Sauce' and can be varied by using sherry or Madeira in place of the brandy. Half wine and lemon juice is equally good; rum and pineapple juice is excellent or, if you don't want to use alcohol, blackcurrant jelly and a little lemon juice is very nice. Use on all sorts of puddings, hot or cold.

Egg Sauce

Add two chopped hard-boiled eggs to half a pint of béchamel. Serve with baked stuffed haddock or cod.

◆ ❖ ◆

This simple sauce is useful to give added nutriment to plain dishes. Nice with steamed or boiled fish as well as baked dishes. Suitable for an invalid diet as a coating for quenelles or steamed fish moulds. It is a good idea to make a lot of roux at once, you can keep it in a jar and use as required; it saves bother when you are in a hurry as you use it for so many purposes.

Fennel Sauce

Add finely-chopped fennel to béchamel sauce and serve with mackerel.

Don't overlook fennel as a garnish, the leaves are so graceful and pretty and make a change from parsley and watercress. Mackerel is a particularly rich fish, and needs something sharp to go with it. Gooseberry sauce (made in the same way as apple sauce) goes well.

Mornay Sauce

Make a béchamel sauce (see page 129), add grated cheese to taste (gruyere and/or parmesan are the best cheeses for this purpose) salt and pepper; then reheat and serve. This sauce can be made richer by the addition of a beaten egg, but in that case you must be very careful not to let it boil after the egg has been added or it will curdle.

◆ ❖ ◆

See notes on cheese sauce, page 131. I like made mustard added to this.

Mayonnaise

This sauce takes about three-quarters of an hour to make; it needs a lot of oil (about 1½ gills) and is essential that the oil be put in very slowly at the start. Put the yolk of an egg in a basin and stir with a wooden spoon until it begins to thicken. Now add olive oil drop by drop. When half finished add salt, vinegar and pepper to taste.

Mayonnaise is tedious to make and I prefer to buy mine bottled, although it is nicer to make your own if you have the time, and if you make a large amount it keeps for ages. The simplest way to add the oil is to cut a wedge-shaped piece out of each side of the cork, the air going in one hole, the oil coming out drop by drop from the other. Keep your basin cool during the mixing process – a wet cloth wrapped round it helps. I add ½ a teaspoon of made mustard when I make mayonnaise and I prefer lemon juice to vinegar.

Sabayon Sauce

1 egg
Sugar to taste
Cooking sherry

Mix all the ingredients together, then whisk until frothy. This can be done beforehand. Immediately before serving, whisk in a double saucepan over a hot heat until light and fluffy all through. This takes about 5 minutes. As soon as you see a trace of thickening at the bottom of the pan, take off the heat and serve.

An interesting sauce can turn the plainest dish into a party one, and this sauce is particularly good for this purpose. For example, cold left-over rice pudding that has gone a bit hard can be rejuvenated if you put it into a fresh dish, sprinkle thickly with sugar and pop under the grill for a moment; served with Sabayon sauce no one would ever recognise it. Always dish a poured sauce separately – as some people may not like it.

Sour Cream Sauce

1 egg
A piece of butter the size of a walnut
½ teacup sour cream
Juice of ½ lemon
A little salt

Whisk the egg with the butter in a saucepan. Put on a low heat and whisk all the time until the butter is melted. Add the lemon juice and mix well. Then add the cream and whisk until it thickens slightly. Be very careful not to let it boil or it will curdle. One of the world's best but least-known sauces.

I would suggest adding the lemon juice after you have taken the pan off the heat (use a double saucepan for heating all egg mixtures). I always add lemon to sauces at the end, as the acid in the lemon is inclined to curdle an egg mixture if it is anywhere near boiling point.

Tomato Sauce

2 lbs. tomatoes
4 medium size onions
A little fat
Salt, pepper

Skin the tomatoes, peel and chop the onions. Melt the fat in a frying pan then add the onions. When golden brown add the tomatoes and cook until soft. Add seasoning to taste.

◆ ❖ ◆

If you want a smooth velvety tomato sauce, sieve your mixture before serving and add a little cream. I use bacon fat for frying the onions and also put a few bacon rinds in the pan with the tomatoes. Celery salt or diced celery improves the flavour too.

Parsley Sauce

Add chopped parsley to béchamel sauce (see page 129).

◆ ❖ ◆

This sauce is a very good way of adding Vitamin C to a dish. Chop your parsley at the last moment to get the maximum vitamin value and don't chop it too fine. The best way to keep parsley (or any green stuff) fresh is to put it unwashed into an airtight jar or covered saucepan.

Redcurrant Sauce

Melt a small pot of redcurrant jelly and add an equal quantity of Worcester sauce. Mix well and serve hot or cold. This sauce is nice with mutton, lamb, ham or tongue.

◆ ❖ ◆

You may find the quantity of Worcester sauce in this recipe a bit high for your liking, if so, dilute with water. Rich meats need an acid sauce to neutralise the fat, hence the custom of serving pork and apple sauce or mint sauce with lamb; this acts in the same way.

CAKES

Demel Krapfen

4 ozs. butter
1½ ozs. caster sugar
6¾ ozs. flour
A drop of vanilla essence
Apricot jam
Chocolate icing

Mix the butter and sugar together, add the flour. Roll out very thin and cut in rounds. Bake for 10-15 minutes on a buttered and floured sheet, in a moderate oven. Do not let them get brown. Make a sandwich of two rounds with the jam in between and on the top. Ice with chocolate icing.

For the icing

3½ ozs. icing or lump sugar
A teacup of water
Just over 4 ozs. chocolate
A little black coffee
A small piece of butter

Boil the sugar with a teacup of water until slightly sticky. Melt the chocolate, pour some of the sugar over it, mix well and gradually add the coffee and butter and the remainder of the sugar and water which is now quite syrupy.

◆ ❖ ◆

When cutting a thin paste into rounds, have a little flour at the side of the board and dip your cutter into this frequently. Press onto the pastry with one sharp cut – don't turn the cutter round as you do so – and remove each round with a floured palette knife. If you keep your biscuits away from the sides and top of the oven they are less likely to overcook. Cool on a wire rack and warm the jam slightly, as it will spread more easily. If you ice while the chocolate is still warm, you can pour it over the biscuits and it will harden quickly with a glossy finish.

Shortbread

4 ozs. butter
2 ozs. sugar
6 ozs. flour

Cream the butter and sugar (it is easiest to do this with your hands). Add the flour gradually. Knead into a smooth ball. Roll out to a quarter inch thick, cut into whatever shape you like and pinch the edges all round. I usually flatten direct into round sandwich tins with my knuckles and do not roll with a rolling-pin, then pinch the edges and cut into six or eight pieces with a knife, so that it is easier to divide when cooked. Do not worry if the paste seems very dry and breakable; it will join up in the oven. Bake in a moderate oven for half an hour. Leave until cold before removing from baking sheet or tin.

In Scotland they add 1 oz. of ground rice to 5 ozs. of flour, this gives a slightly gritty consistency to the shortbread. Personally, I prefer it without. Shortbread should be cut in squares or oblongs about ½ inch thick. Anything thinner is a biscuit. Prick a nice design on the top of the cake with a fork, and decorate with caraway seeds or almonds if you like. The calorie value is high, one small square having 145 calories.

Chestnut Balls

¼ lb. caster sugar
¼ lb. purée of chestnuts
¼ lb. butter
A little cocoa
Some brandy cherries (optional)

Mix the sugar, chestnut purée and butter well together; shape into small balls and roll in the cocoa. You can make the centre of this delicious sweetmeat a brandy cherry, but this is very extravagant unless you happen to have some cherries as the residue of cherry brandy, when it is an excellent way of using them up.

Chestnuts contain a lot of pure starch and very little oil, and are therefore easily digested when cooked. On the continent they are ground and used as flour. To make a chestnut purée, make a slit in the round end of each nut, cover with cold water and boil for 2 or 3 minutes, then draw to the side of the heat and remove the shells and skins. When peeled, simmer in milk and water until tender, about 1½ hours before rubbing through a sieve.

Nut Balls

Just over 4 ozs. caster sugar
Just over 4 ozs. grilled and ground hazelnuts or almonds
2 whites of eggs
A little Demerara or coarse granulated sugar

Mix all together, shape into balls and roll in coarse sugar. Put on a greased sheet in a hot oven and cool off immediately.

◆ ❖ ◆

Don't make the balls too big, about the size of a ping pong ball is best. Although they seem just mouthfuls of crispiness, there is actually a lot of nutriment in them, because nuts are approximately 50% fat and 20% protein.

Ginger Cake

4 ozs. lard or butter
4 ozs. sugar
2 eggs
3-4 tablespoons golden syrup
1 teaspoon ginger
1 teaspoon mixed spice
½ lb. self-raising flour
4 ozs. sultanas or raisins or stem ginger (or more if you like)
A pinch of salt

Cream the lard and sugar, add well-beaten eggs and syrup. Mix ginger, spice and salt with flour and add gradually to the mixture. It is best baked in a flat meat tin lined with greased paper; if a deeper tin is used it will take longer to cook. Bake in a moderate oven for 50-60 minutes.

This is a nice 'gooey' ginger cake, lighter in colour than gingerbread which has bi-carbonate of soda as its raising agent. If you like a strong ginger flavour, double the ground ginger. Melt the syrup slightly to make it easier to mix. When using dried fruit in a cake, blanch with boiling water then leave for a minute or two before rinsing under the cold tap. Dry the fruit in a cloth and dredge with flour, then add with the flour at the end of the mixing. This softens and puffs up the fruit.

Velours Chiffon

2½ ozs. butter
3½ ozs. sugar
7 ozs. chocolate
7 ozs. ground almonds

Beat the butter until soft. Add sugar. Stir very well again. Then add melted chocolate (not too hot) and lastly the almonds. Put in little lumps on a buttered sheet and bake for 20 minutes in a cool oven.

◆ ❖ ◆

It saves a lot of time and labour if you beat the fat in a basin over a pan of hot water. When I first started lo cook I never could understand why you shouldn't melt the butter, but I soon found that I had very sorry results when I did. The reason is that creaming fat and sugar entraps air, which makes your cake rise; you can never get the fluffy whipped cream appearance with oiled fat – there is nothing for it but elbow grease, unless of course, you can get an electric mixer, which will do all the hard work for you.

MISCELLANEOUS

Cheese Biscuits

2 ozs. self-raising flour
3 ozs. grated cheese
Salt, pepper, cayenne if liked
2 ozs. butter
The yolk of an egg

Mix the dry ingredients, add the fat as for pastry. Make into a paste with the yolk beaten up into a little water. Roll out thin and cut into shapes as liked. Bake in a fairly hot oven for 10-20 minutes until crisp and brown.

You will find these a useful standby for cocktail parties; a few caraway seeds sprinkled on the top before baking are good, or you can mix your flour, butter and egg into a dough, roll out in a long strip and spread the cheese over as for jam roly-poly. Roll up and seal, then cut in slices and bake as directed. The result is rather like a catherine wheel and looks most attractive.

Carl Soda Cakes

¼ lb. butter
¼ lb. self-raising flour
¼ lb. mashed potato
1 egg
Salt to taste

Mix the flour, potato and salt; rub in the butter add the egg. Roll into a long sausage, cut into slices and roll each slice into a horseshoe shape with the fingers. Bake in a quick oven for 10-15 minutes. Delicious hot or cold. Can be made croissant size for tea, or tiny (which needs a shorter time in the oven) and rather salty as cocktail savouries. Best eaten the same day.

A richer variation of the Irish Potato Cake. Not only nourishing but a good way to use up your cold mashed potato. It is advisable to put your potato through a ricer, as lumps will spoil the cakes.

Cottage Cheese

Sour milk
Salt, pepper

Leave the sour milk until it has set hard. Put in a saucepan and heat until the whey is separated from the curds. Strain through a square of butter muslin. Tie up and hang to drain for 24 hours. Take out of the bag and work in some salt and pepper. This cheese is improved by the addition of a little sour or fresh cream and/or some butter, and if liked, a little paprika or some finely chopped onion.

The nutritional value of sour milk cheese is the same as milk, as all that is lost is the whey (which is chiefly water) of which milk is 87%. It is not as digestible however, because a chemical change has taken place, hardening the casein which, in fresh milk, is easily broken up by the gastric juices. If a pinch of salt and sugar are worked into the cheese after hanging, it is a good substitute for whipped cream with fruit.

Cream Cheese

Take one quart of fairly thick cream (it must be sweet). Mix well in an enamel bowl. Raise the temperature to 65°-70° F. Add a small teaspoon of junket rennet. Stir for 2 or 3 minutes. Cover the bowl and leave for 1-2 hours until it has coagulated. Then ladle into a coarse linen cloth or huck-a-back towelling and hang up to drain in a cool place for 3 hours. Scrape down outside to middle and vice-versa. Hang up again and repeat every 3 hours until evening. Next morning place between two boards with a 4lb. weight on until of a good consistency. This usually takes about an hour. Salt to taste and mould in grease-proof paper or muslin. One quart of cream will make four to six cheeses of about 4 ozs., each.

An alternative method, which is simpler but takes about 10 days to make, is to hang double cream in a clean wet cloth for 6 or 7 days, and then either proceed with pressing as directed here, or put into a mould lined with muslin and place under a slight pressure for two or three days, turning occasionally daily. Some country people I know wrap their cheese in a wash leather and bury it in the garden for seven days after hanging. It certainly has a fruity flavour, but if you do this, mark the spot or you may find yourself digging up the flower beds to find it!

Brown Homemade Bread

4 ozs. white flour
8 ozs. wholemeal flour
1 level teaspoon salt
2½ heaped teaspoons baking powder
½ pint milk and water mixed

Mix all the ingredients quickly and bake in a very hot oven for 20-30 minutes.

◆ ❖ ◆

In most households there is often an emergency when the bread runs out, so it is a good idea to practise a quick homemade loaf, so that you can knock one off without any qualms when the occasion arises. If you brush your loaves over with milk they will have a nice glossy crust, though the characteristic of this type of bread is a knobbly exterior. This dough is nice baked in little rolls for breakfast. They will take less time to cook if you form into one large loaf, and then cut into twelve portions with a sharp knife.

Ham Rolls

2 handsful mashed potatoes
¼ lb. butter
Yolk of one egg
2-3 handsful flour
Salt
Chopped ham

Mix the potato, butter, salt and egg in a basin. Add flour until the mixture is quite clear of the basin. Knead very well. Roll out then cut into oblongs and fill with chopped ham. Roll up and shape into crescents. Bake in a medium oven first, then in a hot one.

◆ ❖ ◆

When you are using cold mashed potatoes in a pastry dough they must not be too wet or you will put the proportions out. The mashed potato you had for lunch, whipped up with milk and butter, tastes very good but is better used for croquette mixtures. Dry floury potatoes, riced or sieved free of lumps are best for this purpose. Ham rolls are good for picnics or late night snacks.

Potato Scones

Flour
Skinned baked or boiled potatoes
Salt

Mix sufficient flour seasoned with salt to the potatoes to bind them. Roll out, cut into shapes and bake on a greased girdle, or failing that a frying pan. Potato scones must be eaten immediately or they are apt to be heavy.

Serve for tea, split and buttered and wrapped in a napkin, or for breakfast fried in the pan with the bacon. All carbohydrate, they are a good 'filler', but need a protein accompaniment to give them nutritional value.

Pulled Bread

Remove the inside of a loaf of fresh white bread. Pull into small pieces with your fingers. Spread on baking sheets and bake in a very slow oven until hard right through and faintly coloured. Keeps for months in a tin, of course.

This crispy bread is lovely with cheese. The cooking need not be done all at once, as long as the moisture has completely gone during the first baking, so you can save fuel by popping your trays in the oven after cooking the roast or on cake day. If you like French bread sticks, you'll like this.

Red Tomato Sauce

12 lbs. tomatoes	½ oz. cloves
1 lb. sugar	1 lb. dried onion
½ lb. salt	3 ozs. garlic
1 oz. black pepper	4 ozs. shallots
1 teaspoon cayenne pepper	2 lbs. apples
½ oz. allspice	(quartered, but not peeled or cored)

Cover all the above with best vinegar, boil slowly for 4 hours. Strain through a hair sieve when cold. If too thick add more vinegar. Sterilise the bottles and allow them to get cold before filling. Cover and tie down as for jam. This excellent sauce keeps for six to twelve months. The black pepper should be put in a small muslin bag and removed at the end of the boiling. Garlic can be omitted if unobtainable and, of course, ordinary onions peeled and sliced can be used instead of dried ones. If making a smaller quantity than the recipe, 2-3 hours is quite long enough for boiling.

This sauce is more suitable for giving zest to gravies, sauces and soups, than as an accompaniment to meat and fish dishes. Avoid over seasoning any dish to which it is added as it is very strongly flavoured. It is important that the tomatoes used should be sound or it will not keep. Stir the mixture occasionally to prevent catching. This mixture can be cooked in a jar in the oven, or in a preserving pan on the top of the stove. A mixture of one third white vinegar and two thirds brown is best for this purpose.

Tomato Chutney

3 lbs. tomatoes
1 pint vinegar
½ lb. peeled and chopped apples
½ lb. peeled and chopped onions
1 dessertspoon salt
¼ lb. demerara sugar (6 ozs. for green tomatoes)
1½ ozs. pickling spice tied in a muslin bag

Peel and slice the tomatoes. Put into a saucepan with all the other ingredients and boil until tender and thick. Remove the spice and bottle.

◆ ❖ ◆

I think this recipe is improved if you add a few raisins after it is cooked. Don't bottle until several hours after cooking is complete, and stir frequently during cooling process. Although dietetically pickles possess little nutriment, they are useful as a stimulant to the gastric juices and so assist digestion.

Sweet Pickled Cucumber

2 lbs. outdoor cucumber
2 ozs. demerara sugar
½ oz. pickling spice
½ pint vinegar
2 medium-sized onions
Salt

Peel and slice the cucumbers (they should be young ones of about 1 lb. apiece) cover with salt and leave for 8-12 hours. Wash off the salt and put in a saucepan with all the other ingredients. The pickling spice should be put in a little muslin bag and removed before bottling. Boil for 20-30 minutes until the cucumber is tender. Store in glass jars exactly as you would do for jam.

◆ ❖ ◆

Use a lined pan, earthenware jar or iron saucepan for making pickles. I quote from Mrs. Beeton: 'Fatal results have followed the use of copper vessels for pickling purposes', so beware. The best cover is a cork brushed over with melted wax or mutton fat, or some of the patent paper seal now on the market. Keep your pickles in a cool, dry store and examine them occasionally.

Cherry Brandy

4 lbs. morello cherries
4 pints good brandy
3 lbs. loaf sugar

Pick the cherries from the stalks. Put them in a jar with the sugar. The fruit must be fresh and dry. Fill up with the brandy, cover with a bladder and tie down. Cherry brandy should be kept for at least a year, and is better the longer it is kept. Naturally, the better the original brandy used, the better the cherry brandy. When the liqueur has been strained off the cherries can be used in a variety of ways. They are particularly good brought in hot and alight and eaten with ice-cream.

When morello cherries can't be had, an excellent brandy can be made from 1½ lbs. each of black and red cherries, and 1 lb. of raspberries. Some people like a few cloves and a half inch stick of cinnamon added. If the brandy is beyond you, a good cheaper liqueur can be made from gin.

Barley Water

2 quarts boiling water
¼ lb. pearl barley
Yellow rind of 1 lemon
25-30 lumps of sugar
Juice of 3 lemons

Pour boiling water on the barley, lemon peel and sugar. Strain when cold; add lemon juice.

◆ ❖ ◆

Barley water smacks of the sick room, but actually it is a wonderfully refreshing drink in hot weather, especially if it is well flavoured with lemon as in this recipe. I expect you know how important it is to drink enough liquid. Three pints a day at least. If everybody would go on a course of barley water, and give up rich foods for three or four days every now and then, there would be fewer digestive troubles, fewer spare tyres around the waist and better complexions! Barley water ferments quickly, so never keep it over night.

INDEX

Index

Published in 2017 by Unicorn
an imprint of Unicorn Publishing Group LLP
101 Wardour Street
London
W1F 0UG
www.unicornpublishing.org

ISBN 978-1-910787-72-4

10 9 8 7 6 5 4 3 2 1

Designed by Felicity Price-Smith
Printed by Imprint Digital Ltd